VERTICAL LIVING

MIKE HUBBARD

Ark House Press
arkhousepress.com

© 2021 Mike Hubbard

All rights reserved. Apart from any fair dealing for the purpose of study, research, criticism, or review, as permitted under the Copyright Act, no part may be reproduced by any process without written permission.

Unless otherwise stated, all Scriptures are taken from the New International Translation (Holy Bible. Copyright© 1996, 2004, 2007, 2013 by Tyndale House Foundation. Used by permission of Tyndale House Publishers Inc., Carol Stream, Illinois 60188. All rights reserved.)

Some names and identifying details have been changed to protect the privacy of individuals.

Cataloguing in Publication Data:
Title: Vertical Living
ISBN: 978-0-6452860-2-1 (pbk)
Subjects: Christian Living;
Other Authors/Contributors: Hubbard, Mike

Design by initiateagency.com

CONTENTS

Chapter 1	Design	1
Chapter 2	Identity	12
Chapter 3	Relationships	39
Chapter 4	The Journey - Smell The Roses Along The Way	52
Chapter 5	This Moment	56
Chapter 6	Shut Up And Keep Kicking	58
Chapter 7	The Journey Of The Next Step, You Step And God Moves	66
Chapter 8	The Bolting Horse	75
Chapter 9	Love Comes With Boundaries	81
Chapter 10	Mentorship	91
Chapter 11	The Rule Of The 'Last Run'	96
Chapter 12	There Is Always A Price To Be Paid	102
Chapter 13	You're Not A Castle, You're A Temple	117

Chapter 14 The Grief Industry	120
Chapter 15 Are Your Oil Lamps Full?	124
Chapter 16 Grace Will Get You There	128
Chapter 17 World Agendas-The Spirit Of This Age	132
Chapter 18 Go with your Gut.	137
Chapter 19 From Faith To Faith	143
Chapter 20 Celebration	151

ACKNOWLEDGEMENTS

I thank God's grace that has allowed me to come to this point in my life and has privileged me to be able to write this book.

Thank you to 'Ark House Publishing' for stepping in and taking the reins in getting this book out to the community.

I thank my wife Felicity for her constant love and patience, always supporting me along the way.

I give thanks for all my family, friends and patients that have celebrated life with me.

Living this life to my full potential is my ultimate goal.

My hope is to pass on and impart this same hope to all.

FORWARD

Michael Hubbard is a man who knows the importance of being 'well aligned', both physically and spiritually. As a doctor of Osteopathy for nearly forty years he has brought healing relief to countless patients. He invented the 'muscle mate' a massage device that has assisted physical rehabilitation for over thirty years.

Michael is also a credentialed pastor with the Australian Christian Churches (ACC) and a trained counsellor. Both professionally and personally Michael has always aspired to living a full life.

Michael has been happily married to Felicity since 1981 and has a beautifully grown family with three adult children.

In writing this book, 'Vertical Living', Michael's desire is to share life principles he has gleaned from his own life journey and to impart these principles in the hope that they will breathe life into the hearts of those who read this book and in turn have a generational impact.

Michael's prayer is that 'All who read this book would be seekers of the truth, with open hearts and ears to hear'. He says, "There is always a light at the end of the tunnel and if you flip it on its end it will become the eye of the storm." May his wisdom in this book help you see that light and rest and live in the peace found in the eye of the storm!

May you be blessed as you begin your journey of *Vertical Living*!

Pastors Glenn & Clare Wysman

INTRODUCTION

I have spent over 40 years treating people in pain.

As an Osteopath I don't just treat the symptoms of pain but look for and treat the concomitant cause for the pain.

In daily treating the human body, what stands out to me is our amazing design. We are designed to be well and not sick. Pain and sickness are symptoms caused by our fallen world and compounded by us not working within our proper design specifications.

This realization has caused me over the years to look for life principles that support our unique design so we can maintain balance, health, quality longevity, and live life to our full potential.

My hope and prayer for all who read this book, is that the anointing of the Holy Spirit of God will impart into your heart supernatural truths and revelations as on the day of Pentecost.

I pray that as you read, there will be a renewed seed of faith implanted into your heart, and you will tap into this resource and receive the refreshing wellspring of the love of Jesus. That you will be transformed as you read this book by the impartation of God's love, grace, and mercy, and be renewed in mind and refreshed in your spirit.

That you will be empowered to carry on in a walk of faith according to your proper design and grow from strength to strength and glory to glory.

The gift of life is a privilege. With privilege comes responsibility. With this responsibility, we are given Godly authority to be an influence, to be light and salt. To be a pillar of strength and support in your family and community.

Life produces life.

My desire is for all of us to celebrate and dedicate our lives, to live to our full potential in spirit, soul, and body, in Christ. Then pass on the anointing of His love, imparting it to all we meet. Amen.

CHAPTER 1

Design

Why 'vertical living'? Because 'vertical living' is our design. We have been so intricately designed, therefore there is a designer, our Creator. We have been designed and created on purpose for a purpose. We were created out of love and for love. To be in a relationship of love with God and with each other. That is our design and purpose.

The Creator of life lives in a fourth dimensional realm, the realm of Heaven. His Kingdom purpose is to encourage us and to empower us to also live in this Kingdom realm and bring it into the world of our everyday life. In this, we become open vessels of honor, for the God of heaven and earth to download His love, grace and mercy into us and through us.

The Creator becomes our life resource, our fuel, so we can impart and release that same life source into others. As we choose to connect to His resource, we become one with our Creator. (John 17:21-22) We open up into a spiritual intimacy, where we are conceived afresh, 'born again' spiritually.

God becomes our Heavenly Father, Lord and Saviour.

Through this transforming work of the Holy Spirit, we become the influence, the light, the salt, and the change makers in our environment. We become the drawing magnet of His love, to draw others to the vertical plane where His love and life emanate. This 'vertical plane' is the proverbial 'eye of the storm', where peace reigns amid the storms of life. This is where we choose not to get caught up in the vortex of fear and strife. It is the place of our Creator's fourth dimensional reality, the place of 'vertical living'.

HORIZONTAL LIVING IS DIRTY

This worldly place in which we live, and this earthly existence, I call the 'Horizontal' or 'horizontal Living'. It is where our soul, i.e., our mind, will, and emotions, rule our spirit and opens us up to our self-centered, self-serving, prideful egocentric ways. This living can be termed the 'way of the flesh,' also called, our 'carnal nature'. In this sphere of living, we live out of pride, fear, shame, guilt, resentment, unforgiveness, and all forms of controlling and manipulative agendas.

In this environment, we are constantly on guard, on the defensive treadmill of life. We try to protect ourselves from all forms of attacks from others who live on the same horizontal plane. The plane of control, manipulation, fear, envy, jealousy, bitterness, passivity, unforgiveness, anger, self-loathing, and hatred.

God's word tells us that we were made in the likeness and image of our Creator. Genesis 1:26. Then God said, "Let us make man in our own image, according to Our likeness." We were all made in His image-to-image God, to reflect His nature, His character, and His love into the world in which we live. We are created as triune beings. We have a spirit, a soul and a body.

From a worldly or carnal realm, the 'mirror of our soul' does a downward turn. We move away from God and His image and connect with

DESIGN

the image of the 'prince of this world', Satan. Our mirror gets smudged with all the dirt and grime that the flesh, world, and the demonic principalities can throw at us.

We start to see ourselves from this horizontal perspective. In this position we impart this dark and dirty reflection onto ourselves and all those around us. Through this dirty image, we take on an attitude of not just doing wrong but being wrong. Our shame-based nature moves into cover-up and protection mode. We move into the security of denial. We try to prove ourselves through performance.

In this horizontal realm nothing is ever good enough regarding ourselves and the others around us. We stay on the treadmill of always having to try harder to accept ourselves and others. So, satisfaction and acceptance are always very fleeting.

SPIRITUAL WARFARE NEEDS TO BE FOUGHT SPIRITUALLY

It is understandable that in horizontal living, we get exhausted and irritable and take it out on ourselves and everybody around us - because, we are all 'the enemy'. We try to keep fighting with weapons of self-destruction where everybody loses.

It is essential to remember (Ephesians 6:12) "For we do not fight against flesh and blood but against principalities and powers". This war is called 'SPIRITUAL WARFARE'. It has been waged by Satan and all the fallen entities even before man fell from grace. This warfare will carry on until the second coming of Jesus Christ. It is only from 'putting on Christ' (Romans 13:14) putting on the soldier's uniform and enlisting in God's army, can we fight the good fight (1 Timothy 6:12) in His power and authority.

Unfortunately, man's nature, from living in the horizontal does not cut it. It is a feeble reflection because we can only reflect our fallen nature, with all the damage, griefs, pains, sicknesses, and sorrows that are the side effects of man's fall from grace.

THE WAY FORWARD- CHRIST IN US

Our restoration back into God's image can only be done through receiving into our hearts His only begotten son, Jesus Christ, as our Lord and savior. God came to earth in the flesh as a man, lived a sinless life, and fulfilled all biblical prophecies to fulfill God's word.

He then suffered and died on the cross for our sins and then was resurrected on the third day so that we could have eternal life with God through accepting Jesus as God the Son, our Lord, and Savior. Jesus then entered heaven and gave us His Holy Spirit so that we could impart His love, grace, and mercy to all.

We are then 'born again' and carry this transformed reflection of our true selves into this world. Then we have, "Christ in us the hope of Glory" (Colossians 1:27).

This terminology of being born again speaks of spiritual conception. It means we open the door of our spiritual heart to God, Rev (3:20), and the Spirit of God comes in and impregnates His Spirit into our spirit. We have at that time received God's spiritual chromosomal DNA. We then, like the fetus, grow, mature, and change through all of life's difficulties into the nature and character of Christ Jesus.

So, we are able to mirror Jesus, as His character and nature forms in us, and reflect him into the world.

This purpose came out of God loving us and wanting to relate and be in a relationship with us. Working in our proper design, we then mutually desire to be in a vertical relationship with Him. This is our correct design to function out of His love and purpose.

Because we have been made in God's image, we have been given our own will to make our own choices, to prioritize our position, vertical or

DESIGN

horizontal. It is like tapping into the right fuel resource. One is empowering and unlimited - the other fuel resource is disempowering, limited, and damaging.

Unfortunately, man's choice through Adam and Eve caused them to choose the way of Satan! Hell was never meant for man but only meant for the fallen angels. Man, through sin, chose Satan's destiny.

God's love expressed through salvation became the only way and answer to save man from his bad choices. Unfortunately, man's choice caused a spiritual divide between man and God, causing man to feed off the wrong resource. The resource of fear, shame, knowledge, and power.

These flesh resources drain us to exhaustion, promoting bad attitudes and agendas and all forms of defensive control. We try to hide and protect our damaged nature, which causes damaged people to damage other people.

ASK GOD TO BE YOUR BUSINESS PARTNER

The vertical living positioning is where we choose to come back into our true nature of being sons and daughters of God. Then we understand that our design is about God and about His business in us. We are then aligned with His Kingdom's purpose in us. As Jesus said in Luke 2:49, "Did you not know, I must be about my Father's business." This position enhances a life of love, joy, peace, and patience, healing, empowerment, and freedom.

Think of it like the Star Trek movies where captain Kirk positions himself and says, "beam me up, Scotty". That is our proper place and position to be beamed up into communion with God in Heavenly places, (Ephesians 2:6), "and raised us up together and made us sit together in the heavenly places in Christ Jesus."

ASK, SEEK, KNOCK

How do we get to this vertical reality? It always comes from a heart position of seeking, asking, and knocking (Matthew 7:7) and doing it every day.

At the age of eleven I had a sense of life's greatness and bigness and I wanted to find out more. My favorite song at that time, which was in the mid 1960s was 'What's it all about Alfie'. That was my ongoing question for many years. Having a heart to seek after truth puts you on the path to the vertical.

A scripture where God shows us the path to take, to connect with Him, is in Jeremiah 29:13, "And you will seek Me and find Me, when you search for Me with all your heart."

People will only find the vertical if they have the heart to seek after it, to seek after God with all their heart. Human nature can be likened to a cell structure. Being designed in God's image. Scripture speaks of human beings being 'children of light (Ephesians 5:8).

The drawing below depicts our human design in the image of a cell. A 'light cell'.

DESIGN

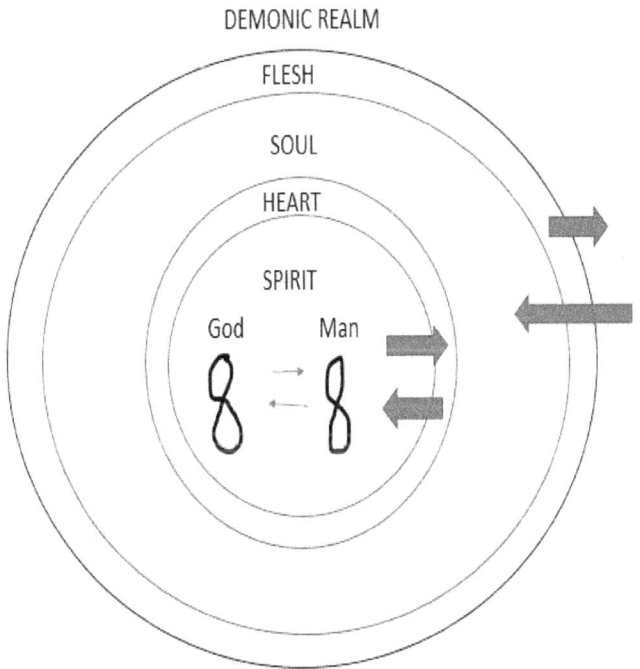

This cell drawing depicts our design. We have a spirit, soul, i.e., (mind, will, emotion) we have a heart. The heart is like a semi-permeable cell membrane of the spirit nucleus. In essence the spiritual heart is our 'spiritual compass', causing us to either draw to the things of the spirit or the things of the soul. The outside surface of the soul is the 'flesh'. The flesh nature has been made toxic through the fall of man.

When Adam and Eve moved into unbelief and disobeyed God, they took on the toxic nature of Satan. Thus, man was infected with his evil intent and his destiny as an enemy of God.

This flesh nature then became influenced by this dark nature of evil. Like this human cell analogy, the flesh nature is semi-permeable to the outside world of toxic darkness and evil, self-serving intent. This evil intent, if allowed, will then invade our souls and play havoc with our life force spiritually, physiologically, emotionally, and physically. It can lead to distress, debility, and eventual destruction.

WORKING OUTSIDE DESIGN LEADS TO BREAKDOWN

If our flesh nature is allowed to take over our being, we become insatiable for all the bad evil influences and stimulants of life. Like all forms of self-gratification, it can never be satisfied. We always want more and more until it kills us or others.

Our 'light cell' becomes darkened, toxic and dies.

We continually try to fill the gaping void of dissatisfaction that can never be filled. Only the love of God can fill the void. All other influences that we grab onto simply medicate our damaged souls but can't protect us against the damaging nature of the void.

Every design badly used breaks down. We express this damage through the insatiable side effects of sex, drugs, 'rock and roll', power plays, performance, fear, shame, unforgiveness, control, anger, hatred, resentments, pride, ego etc., which are all symptoms of this void.

Our entire world is based on relationships. We live, breathe, move and have our being expressed through relationships. The problem is that the whole world struggles in living out of relationships, especially good relationships, or more importantly, God relationships.

You see, our heart and soul are designed to be filled with the light and the love of God. Without that filling, we have a void. Voids by nature must be filled. And like the song says, we will be 'looking for love in all the wrong places.'

Good relationships grow love and community. Bad relationships do the reverse, growing fear, hatred, isolation, and death. We are all crying out to know how to do relationships better. Better understanding, better listening, better heart agendas. Right now, who are you and I serving and honoring at this moment in time?

If you are serving yourself or somebody else's agenda at this moment in time, you are most probably living out of the horizontal plane. Horizontal living is you looking and dealing with your agendas and desires and or dealing with somebody else's desires and plans. That is the horizontal 'tug of war'.

The 'good news' says that "God is love"; (1 John 4:8). Anyone who does not love does not know God because God is love. God also says in Matthew 22:37-40 in summary, "Love God and love your neighbor as yourself," in that order. In this order, we can tap into God's love first. This love is our fuel resource which heals, empowers, and brings transformational change. But it comes at a price - here it is. (Rom 12:1-2) **Living Sacrifices to God.** "I beseech you therefore, brethren, by the mercies of God, that you **present your bodies a living sacrifice, holy, acceptable to God,** which is your reasonable service. And do not be conformed to this world, but **be transformed by the renewing of your mind**, that you may prove what is the good and acceptable and perfect will of God."

God's heart's desire is for all to know Him and to love him. That is His Kingdom purpose.

The question is then, how do we get to do that, to know Him and to love him? By meeting Him in the plane of His love, that is the vertical plane where we can ask Him to receive His love.

The journey to the vertical, the fourth dimensional plane, must come from a place of belief and prayer.

BELIEF + ACTION = FAITH

Belief plus action moves you into the dimension of faith. Prayer is acting on that belief by believing that you are communicating with a Heavenly Father who loves you and wants to commune with you and wants to be in a functional and genuine relationship with you - the child who he loves.

His love came down from heaven, John 3:13 - Jesus, "the Son of man."

In the Gospel of Luke 24:13, Jesus in His resurrected body appears and walks and talks with two disciples as they are walking on a road. These two disciples are walking away from Jerusalem, away from their purposes in God.

Jesus talked with them along the journey and explained to them His revelations, truths, and God's desires and hopes for their lives. This is the same for us. We can walk in the garden of life with Jesus any time, day or night and receive His thoughts, His mind, His revelation and His love for each of us. Through this we move more into our full potential and future.

As with the disciples walking to Emmaus, they received the revelation of God's love and purpose for them. So, they turned back to Jerusalem and back to their destiny in God.

You can have the same revelation even now. Ask Jesus to give you the revelation, the understanding, and the knowledge of His love for you. Remember, "Ask, and you shall receive." God does not lie. If you struggle trusting, ask for God's love to fill you afresh that you can choose to trust and believe.

If you struggle to believe in God and want to know if God is real then decide to seek after God's truth with all your heart. God's word is evident in Jeremiah (29:13), "And you will seek me and find me when you search for me with all your heart."

If you don't believe, but you agree that your belief system, whatever it may be, could be wrong, then say, "God, if you are real, soften my heart that I can receive your truth." If you are not a seeker after truth, you won't find the truth and will never experience the reality of complete love and freedom.

DESIGN

You can hold on to your pains and grievances. You will stay in your state of unforgiveness, willful denial, and your many forms of defensive control. But your inner heart knows, there is a God.

I ask you with deep sincerity for the saving of your soul, to cover all your bases' and ask, "Well God if you are real, soften my heart so I can ask for the heart to seek after your truth." In doing this simple asking, the beauty is that you've got nothing to lose and everything to gain. So have a go - just for the sake of seeing what's around the corner, you will see the vista of God's love, grace and mercy. 'You'll never know if you don't have a go'. ☺

The positive outcome will be that you will be filled afresh through His presence, with the fuel of life, His Love.

CHAPTER 2

Identity

FROM PERFORMANCE TO PEACE

I was brought up in a loving family where my grandparents lived with us for seven years and lived next door to us for the next seven years. There were six children in the family, two sets of boy twins and two sisters. I was one of the elder twins.

Because of the size of the family and being an elder sibling, we were given many duties and chores to do around the home, including cleaning dirty nappies, as disposables had not been invented at that stage. However, I won't go into that as I am still recovering from bad memories, as you can imagine!

Being one of the eldest, performing duties and discipline was very important to the family. There was a sense of pride and acceptance through being applauded through performance. This even carried on in early school years.

When I was in first-class my mother and grandmother had taught us many songs. I would go with my twin brother into many different

IDENTITY

classrooms performing these songs. We also had a tennis court in the backyard, and I became a proficient tennis player.

THE PERFORMANCE TRAP

My parents and grandparents used to watch me playing tennis competition from the kitchen window. Then, after the set there would be the ongoing dissecting of the performance in how to do better.

Performance is acceptable, but if it becomes your life as a way of proving yourself, it can become very tiring and exhausting and can even lead to burnout if not properly controlled. This was my case, as I started to put more and more pressure on myself to perform more and do better.

So, at the age of sixteen, through burn out, I stopped playing tennis. It was due to the stress I put on myself to be continually applauded, loved, and accepted. You see, I was already loved and accepted. But, my flesh nature, based on shame, guilt and fear would not allow myself to believe that I was already special, and I did not need to perform any more to prove myself.

This flesh nature, which we are born into does not allow us to have a true sense of our own special and unique character. Our self-esteem has many holes in it; through fear and negative thinking, it deflates very quickly.

Unfortunately, the treadmill of finding my own 'flesh identity', caused me not to learn my lesson. I went from a budding tennis career to a budding acting career.

Of course, my need to perform and achieve in the acting arena, to be applauded and accepted, only increased.

So, now my sights shifted to performing on the 'world stage' of acting. So, my sights got higher and grander, as did the ongoing pressure.

After a few years of acting school and getting small parts, the first inkling of a change in my heart started to take shape and come into my life. I met Felicity.

Felicity was seventeen, as 'cute as a button 'with the most beautiful smile. I was twenty-one and smitten. Funny enough, we had met at a country tennis tournament in Bega. By this stage I had changed my attitude to tennis and was not so intense.

Our first meeting was unforgettable as we were all in a motel room with friends playing a card game called wink. If you received the Jocker card, you could wink people out of the game. As it would happen, I got the 'Joker' about five times in a row, I spent practically the whole night winking at Felicity, and it worked!

By the time I was twenty-three I was still acting but subtle changes were coming in, 'love changes'. Loving Felicity started to take over from loving myself.

I had a 'revelation'. I believe revelation can come to us through people who pray for us. Where God's grace starts to trickle in and soften the 'soil of our heart' and life seeds begin to germinate in our hearts. Then, we are able to see with more clarity and enlightenment through God's perspective.

In my case, I realized that I didn't know if I could be a good husband and a good father and still be an actor? Acting and performing were still all about me and me being my own God and that I was the center of my universe.

I realized that choosing love and marriage would have to cause me to be selfless rather than selfish. It was a new ball game entirely.

My spiritual journey was still in progress. It went from the question of 'What's it all about?', when I was eleven years old, to a statement when I was nineteen. This statement went like this. -----

"Well God if you are real, you better remove the barrier so I can see the truth, because I can't see it."

IDENTITY

I may have been more frustrated about life at the time, but I still had a seeking heart, thank goodness. A good scripture to back this up says, "My Grace is sufficient for you, for my strength is made perfect in weakness" (2 Corinthians 12:9).

Because of my nature and human nature generally, we quite often must get to the end of ourselves, to the point of exhaustion, where we hopefully cry out for help. Yet, for many of us, we willfully choose not to ask for help. Anxiety, depression and even suicide can be the end result. I pray we all cry out sooner than later.

The prayer factor, 'going to the vertical', was still kicking in from other resources. An example was Felicity's mother took both of us to a Billy Graham crusade at Randwick Sydney in 1979. I remember her looking at me and saying, "Michael, would you like to go forwards and give your life to Jesus"? I, of course, in my not so humble way, said, "No thank you. I think I am a good enough person." I now cringe at the statement, but I was twenty-three years of age and still my own God.

Sowing and reaping is a universal principle. It can only be altered through improving the nature of the soil that the seed grows in. if not, you are destined to have repeated outcomes leading to continued negative consequences and damage. This was shown clearly in my father.

My father was a quality man, a quiet man, and he was very reserved and honorable. He was a solicitor bringing up a family of six children. He struggled with his own sense of worth and self-image and did courses such as 'mind dynamics' and 'leadership dynamics'. They were mind-altering courses that try to change your natural qualities, and for my reserved, gentle father, it was like being hit with a sledgehammer.

He had a nervous breakdown. He spiraled into self-hatred, rejection, and the oblivion of depression. He separated from my mother for three to six months, left his legal practice, and took up smoking.

He did come back into the marriage and life, but he kept carrying some of his grief and damage with him. He was always a good, gentle man, he carried great wisdom and always had a heart for helping others.

THE BEGINNING OF THE KGFI MOTTO

I have a motto, (KGFI) **'keep going for it'**. It was attributed to the go-getting nature of my mother. Having to raise six children was always going to be a hard task. My mother, whom I call the 'life enhancer' would always find ways of making ends meet. Firstly, with her cooking.

As I was the eldest with my twin brother, we were always six hungry kids - there was always the hunt for food in the pantry. We would always ask, "What's for dinner?" Mum's answer would always come back, "Bread and look at it." But like a magician, Mum would always miraculously manifest meals out of nowhere.

For fitness, Mum took up Hatha yoga. When finances became a problem, she fixed the problem by becoming a yoga teacher. She taught yoga classes in a separate rumpus room in our backyard for the next eleven years.

Mum was always a bit of a 'fixit' type of person. She would always have a go. Would never give up, and always gave her best and encouraged us to do the same. She became a very competitive tennis player and a bridge player, even into her eighties.

When I was fifteen, my grandparents went around Australia by caravan for 11 months. They came back with eight old oil drums full of gemstone rocks. Mum decided to keep my grandparents busy when they got back home. She set up some lapidary equipment, and then encouraged them to turn those rough rocks into gemstones.

A bit like what God does with us!

IDENTITY

Mum, at this time, was selling French perfume at the international airport duty-free store. She realized that she was good at sales, which she was. she could 'sell ice to Eskimo's'.

My mother then got the brain wave to buy opals and jewelry settings. She would ask my aunty and grandparents to set those stones into the settings. Mum would then on-sell opal jewelry to the duty-free store and then sell them out of the same store. Good Gig Mum!

Thus, began her very successful opal jewelry company called 'Opalana Jewelry. This was a real winner financially and took the pressure off dad. Well done, Mum.

By this stage in my life, I decided to leave acting and that lifestyle and find another career. I started working in and managing health food stores. I also began studying courses in holistic medicine and eventually went to full-time study as a Naturopath and an Osteopath.

My father was still trying to cope with life. He would smoke four packets of 'capstan 'cigarettes a day, eating large blocks of craft cheese in one go, and three kilo blocks of dark chocolate. He also was eating half inch slabs of peanut butter on his toast and copious amounts of coffee.

I remember asking him one day, "Hey dad, if you knew that in three months you were going to die, but if you stopped your smoking and all your bad habits, that you would be OK, would you do it?"

He pondered for a while and then said, "I would have to think about it." Nine months later in February 1981, at the age of forty-nine, my dad died from a massive heart attack.

My Dad made his choice. His burnout through the years of 'sowing and reaping', created too much chronic stress. He had nothing left in the tank except a lot of inflammation in his blood vessels and too much cholesterol on his arterial walls.

However, the shock of losing my Dad at such a young age didn't deter my Mum, but spurred her on.

Several years down the track, she would put an ad in the personal ad column in the newspaper. She would meet many suiters on her veranda - one of these suiters became her second husband. Ian Giles.

Mum had bought land at Mona Vale in Sydney and started to build a new home. The now Mrs. Giles got involved in a community dispute over nearby land that was meant to be a local park for children. In fighting for this park, Mum became a fighting crusader. She was also very good at that too. When it came to the needs in the local community, she 'had no fear'.

Her mothering instincts took on a whole new level, a community level. It included her being involved with the setting up of a new council. This eventuated, of course because Mum fought for it. It became Pittwater Council. She became one the first counsellors in Pittwater Council and was in council for twenty years - Deputy mayor for five years and Mayor of Pittwater for seven years.

Scripture speaks of persevering, enduring, "fighting the good fight and running the good race to the finish line and keeping the faith" (2Timothy 4:6-7). This would be Mum's catch phrase.

Mum became not only a life enhancer at home, but for the whole community. Oh, by the way, that original park that caused mum to become a community crusader, is now called, 'Patricia Giles Park'. "Well done good and faithful servant (Matthew 25:21) (KGFI) Well done Mother!

Back to my dad and me.

My Dad, in some respects, I think he was trying to prove himself from a typical upbringing of not being fully accepted by his own father. His Father was often very critical and not a good communicator.

In a subtle way, I had probably been experiencing a similar relationship, with my father. Not that my dad was critical, he just wasn't a very good communicator with his feelings and thoughts. He was naturally reserved. It is interesting how some generational influences go down the

IDENTITY

line. Still with the right approach to our responses, these influences can be circumvented, and we can alter our direction and future. Fortunately, we have a heavenly Father who is a great communicator.

With the death of my Father, I became more fervent in seeking after truth.

I met some friends when I was doing my Osteopathic studies. They were followers of Jesus and would meet in the park at lunch times for a Bible study and I would venture down to join in. One day they asked me to go to a concert at the Town Hall.

This concert ended up being a gospel outreach. The worship music caused me to by-pass all my questionings and took me straight to the throne room of God, where the truth of Jesus Christ as Lord and Savior impregnated my searching heart. This meeting was held in August 1981. I told Felicity, "I must go forwards and receive Jesus as my Lord and Savior." I did!

We were driving home, and the revelation of God changed me, Felicity and I were engaged by this stage in our journey but there had not been a set time for our marriage. But once receiving the Lord and the indwelling of the Holy Spirit, it seemed clear to me whom I was serving and honoring. Suddenly I was no longer the center of my life, Jesus was.

His truth and purpose were in me. Even though I had had no church background in my whole life, I suddenly knew what to do. I said to Felicity, "I have to live a life to honor God now and not myself. Let's get married as soon as we can get a reception organized." That was August 1981 - we were married by December 1981. Prayer can take a while, but God moves fast! 1981 was a big year.

In 1983 our daughter Angie had been born. By the time Angie was three years and three months old, our two sons Philip and Jeremy had also arrived. I had taken over a very busy Osteopathic practice in Parramatta. I was living in faith but not really by faith and within two years, I was burnt out. The generational performance trap had hit home again. The good news this time was that I had a new resource to tap into; I just had to learn how to use it.

YOU ARE NO LONGER A CIVILIAN

I knew I had received the Holy Spirit and knew He was my helper and my counsellor and would lead me into all truth, wisdom and understanding. It is important to realize that when you gain faith and the knowledge of Jesus Christ as your Lord and Savior, you need to change your spiritual clothes. It is like when a man or woman enlists in the army. Straight away, when you enroll, you put on an army uniform. You are no longer a civilian, and you are no longer in Kansas Dorothy - As in the story of "The Wizard of Oz" Where Dorothy's perception of reality changed when she ventured into the Land of Oz.

Being a soldier, you are trained and disciplined in how to take orders from your commander. You are trained to be strategic, and you are always ready to take on the enemy. "To put on Christ", (Romans 13:14) that is your new soldier's uniform, you are not meant to take it off.

If you do take off your uniform in Christ, you're back into civilian mode where you don't listen or take commands very well. In this civilian state of mind, you are generally not strategic, and when the enemy comes in to attack you, civilians normally don't stand and fight; they run away and hide. With a soldier's anointing and mentality and authority, we have the power to stand and fight. We can 'hold the line', to claim back the land that the enemy has taken from us, our family, and our generations.

Scripture is clear – If we are not obedient to God's commands, we can open ourselves up to all sorts of damage. This damage can have a negative influence on our spirit, soul, body, and our families, to the "third and fourth generation" (Exodus 34:7). But in Christ we have the victory that has already been won for us on the cross at Calvary. The

IDENTITY

victory is ours - we just need to appropriate our authority every day and take the ground.

Throughout all history, the essence and principle of being a good soldier is that he has already taken on the position of being dead to himself. His only function and purpose is to honor and obey the orders of the commander. As it is written in (1 Corinthians 15:31) "I die daily."

I realized that I had a new heart and a desire for the work of helping people in pain. However, I also realized I didn't have the right nature for the work. I still had my old flesh nature, with a civilian attitude.

In many ways, I had put the Holy Spirit 'on the shelf'. I was still working out of my old nature. My nature was too intense, empathetic, sensitive, and I didn't like responsibility. A fine actor but a lousy Osteopath. Sorry, all you actors, it was my bag, not yours!

As a health practitioner, I felt I was responsible for fixing people. That's a lot of pressure to take on yourself every day.

My concerns grew and I became more anxious about having to perform and having to be more responsible.

It became an endless cycle of stress and anxiety.

I didn't even want to get out of bed in the morning. I would wake up every morning saying, "Why me Lord? I can't do this."

I would be looking forward to the relief of the calming respite of weekends. Unfortunately, the weekends would come, and I couldn't enjoy them because I was thinking about the stress of Monday mornings. The same scenario would happen in the holidays.

I realized that I was not enjoying the gift of 'the moment' and realized I was wasting my life by not enjoying each moment as a special gift.

"I WANT YOU TO WASH MY FEET"

At this stage, I had what I would call a 'spiritual dream'. To me, a spiritual dream is a dream that has such a reality stamped on it that it is crystal clear with a crystal-clear message that you never forget. This was one of those dreams.

In this dream, God spoke to me. He said, "I want you to wash my feet." The following image in this dream was the Lord looking like a big white statue. I had a yellow bucket of water and a sponge. I knelt before this white statue and started washing the feet.

As I was washing this statue, I had a sense of me doing a good job. Then all of a sudden, the white material that the statue was made out of started to crumble away. The more I tried to fix it up, the worse it was getting.

The next image was me on a high hill looking down on this statue that had degenerated into a skeletal mess. I started to cry out, "What have I done wrong, what have I done wrong?" As I said this, suddenly all this white material started flying through the air past me and reforming back on the statue, making it bigger and better than ever. That was the end of the vision in that dream.

Straight away there were two clear points that came to me.

1/ I needed to humble myself before the Lord, and
2/ In my humbling I would be used to help heal the body of Christ.

Within days I started to see more Christian patients. With God's love, grace, and mercy, and my willingness, the Lord did a sanctifying and transforming work on my soul through His amazing partnership with me.

His extraordinary grace is available for all of us to bring in change and transformation every day. We all need a warfare strategy with discipline to bring in this transforming change. I asked God to download to me His battle plan strategy. I got it! Today, thirty-eight years later, I still use this strategy.

IDENTITY

'VERTICAL LIVING' IS 'THE PRINCE AND PRINCESS POSITION'. WE ARE SONS AND DAUGHTERS OF GOD

The Prince and Princess position was formulated out of necessity. 'Necessity is the mother of invention'. So, the necessity was born out of my burnout.

By this stage, I had a young growing family, so I had to either get another career or I had to sort out my attitude and 'get on with it'. The best way to get on with it is to pray.

As I prayed a verse came to me from (Luke 2:49), where Jesus said, "Did you not know that I must be about my Father's business?" Wow!

The revelation came to me like a lightning bolt. It was this, "Whatever is going on in your life, it is **none of your business. We are in partnership with God, and it is His business.** God our Heavenly Father, the Creator of all things is also my daily business partner. You see I was used to doing everything on my own and for myself. I was and always felt that I had to be responsible.

I realized that at the end of the day that God is ultimately responsible for outcomes. All we can do, as I used to say to my kids is "do your best and let God look after the rest".

I realized that we can't possibly be responsible for outcomes. That's 'above our pay grade'. That's God's domain. What we can do is to be accountable to give our best every day with what we have to give.

I could do that, but now without all the unreasonable pressure that wasn't mine to take on. That's the same for all of us. What a relief.

With this positioning we can all start to enjoy life more and stay in the place of peace rather than in the exhausting vortex of over performance.

I now realized my only real responsibility was to give any new information I had to my Heavenly business partner. Of course, you would do the same thing for an earthly business partner, it is proper business etiquette. So why would you not have the same etiquette and business sense to involve your Heavenly business partner in all things?

The revelational position that came to me was this:

> **"I am a son of the King; and I am about the King's business."**

We are all sons and daughters of the King (2 Corinthians 6:18) and princes and princesses of the Kingdom. Therefore, our position is totally related to who we are in Christ, not in who we are in the world, not in what we do or how well or how bad we do it.

Being a prince or a princess is your proper position. Performance becomes irrelevant to your role in who we are in Christ. We don't need to perform to gain position or maintain a position to be ok.

Our spiritual bloodline is that once we except Jesus Christ as God the Son, our Lord, and Savior, we are truly born again into Christ as sons and daughters of God. This is our eternal position which can never be altered or taken away. How relieving and releasing was that revelation to me. It can also be for you.

GAUGING THE FRUIT OF THE SPIRIT

Like a beautiful plant, we are watered by the love of God through the daily outpouring of the Holy Spirit. All we have to do is ask and believe and receive that outpouring of His love into our spirit. We then continue to grow and mature day by day in the likeness and the nature and the character of Christ. This is shown in us and through us in the form of the fruit of the Spirit.

We produce in our life through the growing and releasing of the fruit of the Spirit in us, giving it out to all who would receive this fruit. All fruit grows from being watered. We are saturated by God's love every day, if we are open to it.

IDENTITY

The important point in this is to be able to receive God's love.

Sometimes through emotional traumas, we can move into spiritual droughts. The soil of our hearts can be hardened. In this, at times, it is hard for that life-giving water to penetrate. Pray for God's love to soften the soil of your heart.

Often, we need the softening agent of repentance and forgiveness to bring in the necessary breakthrough to soften our damaged hearts. "The fruit of the Spirit is Love, Joy, Peace, Patience, kindness, goodness, faithfulness, gentleness and self-control. Against such there is no law." (Galatians 5:22-23) This equals 'FREEDOM' from the world and all its constraints and prejudices.

As we release the heavenly fragrances of the fruit of the Spirit, our environment changes, and we change environments. The releasing of such fruit into our life and the lives around us then releases the seeds of such fruit. When released they will then produce more fruit in all the lives that receive such fruit that will continue to multiply. How exciting is that!

It is important to remember (Matthew 12:33), "Either make the tree good and its fruit good, or else make the tree bad and its fruit bad; for a tree is known by its fruit.

My prayer is that it will be the same for you.

CHANGE YOUR POSITION

My next question was, how do I implement this spiritual position into my living reality? There was another scripture I remember in (1 Corinthians 15:46) "However, the spiritual is not first, but the natural, and afterward the spiritual."

So, to start, I needed to make a change in my attitude. I decided that I needed to reset my position. I would breathe tall, do some shoulder shrugs, do a few more deep breaths and do this for thirty seconds approximately every hour. I would do this reset just before I would see my next patient.

So as a general rule of thumb, this spiritual repositioning is a thirty second reset physically mentally emotionally and spiritually every hour.

KEEP SHORT ACCOUNTS

By keeping short accounts this way, you give no room for the enemy, i.e., Satan and his demonic cohorts, can't get any foothold against you through you having a bad attitude. Therefore, there is no producing bad fruit. By doing this, you are constantly repositioning yourself in God and using your God-given authority through prayer, and mindfulness, into whatever situation you or a loved one is in. You are then using your authority in word and action as a Prince and Princess of the Kingdom. You are opening your heart door to Jesus and closing all soulish and flesh doors, keeping the enemy out.

As your heart door opens to the Spirit of God, His life resource pours into your soul and brings in a transformational change where your character is progressively being molded into the character of Christ.

A nice add-on benefit is you can see and experience all the fruit of the Spirit as you continue to grow. How sweet it is.

My thinking was that by keeping short accounts I could 'nip in the bud' any open door that may allow for any negative stress and demonic influence to enter in.

CHANGING POSTURE ENHANCES WELL BEING

As I breathed tall, there was an instant change in my posture. I felt instantly more energized from my physical change as a tall posture takes a lot of pressure off the spine, the nervous system, and the lungs. Changing

IDENTITY

to a tall posture also reduces stress hormones and releases more feel-good hormones. These postural changes also boost the immune system.

This was the first step in the change. The next step was to assess my soulish, attitudinal position and my spiritual position. I was checking in on my fruit, was it good or bad, and where was it coming from?

So, to bring that into a cognitive context I asked myself this question to assess my attitude:

At this moment do I have Love, Joy, Peace and Patience,
and if not then why not?

They are the first four fruits in the nine fruits of the Spirit, (Galatians 5:22)

Love

If you are struggling with love, you're using your own limited love resource and not God's. Scripture is clear that our flesh nature is in enmity (Romans 8:7) against our spirit man. It's called spiritual warfare.

Our own love nature is very limited in its capacity to be selfless. Our limited capacity is like a fuel resource with many 'holes in the bucket'. No matter what the relationship we have with one another, we soon become more and more selfish, unsatisfied, angry, and bitter. We soon dry up and get more brittle and relationships crumble.

THE GRASS IS GREENER WHERE YOU WATER IT

Loving relationships are like having a beautiful plant - it can only grow and bear fruit if you constantly water it. With our 'flesh love', we don't only stop watering, but we start looking for greener grass.

With our selfish desires taking over, we become blind to the reality of what is going on, not realizing that 'the grass is always greener where you water it'.

As a result, we can wander into other paddocks of envy, lust, and self-gratification, which can never be satisfied. We can trespass onto foreign soils of discontent and do damage on properties that are not ours.

God's love is sacrificial. Therefore, with His love, we can put our lives on the altar of life and choose to trust our Heavenly Father in the soils where he has placed us to prosper.

Scripture is clear that to function in God's love, we are to 'die daily'. Just like when the seed is planted in the ground, in the dark soil that can encompass us with despair, hurts and griefs, the seed must die to itself so it can be changed and transformed into something much greater than itself, and through that, to bear much fruit. (1Corinthians 15:31). To die daily to our will and choose God's will. Jesus said, "Not as I will but as you will" (Matthew 26:39). In this we tap into a wellspring of overflowing love that is sacrificial and selfless by nature and never runs dry.

No more brittle plants and relational droughts; praise God. But remember, effort and discipline are the cost. Everything in life comes at a cost and 'there is always a price to be paid', sometimes sooner, sometimes later.

Paying the love price of choosing God's will is sacrificial by nature and therefore generally painful in one form or another. But it is so worth it. At the end of the day, it is the only strategy that works by design. Ask God daily to fill you afresh with His Love. He will do it.

DON'T BE A DRIED OUT SPOUNGE

I remember a time in my life, I felt like a dried-out sponge - there was nothing left in the tank. All I could do was to ask God every day to help me to be able to receive and fill me with more of His Love. This request lasted three months. Then, one day I was at a camp with some youth.

In the past, I would be looking at attitudes and judging and looking for fault. But suddenly, I just wanted to laugh with them, play games, have fun and accept them and love them just as they were. A miracle had taken place through God's drip affect on the garden of my heart. The same can happen to your heart right now. As Jesus did in the garden at Gethsemane, under the pressure of death, he chose God's will over his own - "Not my will but yours be done."

Ask God to water your heart with His love. Choose his will over yours, and in good time, the fruit of His love will come.

Joy

Unfortunately, the world has gone down the self-gratification track to fill up the godless void in life. Feelings and happiness, which are valid emotions, have been unfortunately upgraded into idols of life. People will expend all their energies, money and soul on the altar of self-gratification to maintain these feelings and to medicate against the pain of the void.

This form of medication, through stirring up the froth and bubble of life cannot last and must dissipate. Like any addiction, we want to fill the void more and more, but the satisfaction disappears in a moment. So, our human flesh nature stirs up as much froth and bubble it can, e.g., partying, music, sex, drugs, alcohol, all forms of sports, entertainment, adornments, money property, power, prestige etc.

All these positions and activities are of value in the proper context of life. But if they are used to medicate against the pain of life or to cover up and protect us from degrees of damage, then we will through exhaustion tend to do more and more damage, to ourselves and others. For all these substitutes can be a spiritual counterfeit.

I think it is always important to discern what is your "first love", (Revelation 2:4) as idol worship can always pop up around the corner.

I remember when I first got saved, I struggled with the idea of giving up certain habits. But as we keep persevering and enduring in choosing God as our first love, we get transformed as His character forms in us.

There is the old story about the guy who falls off a cliff - he grabs a branch and is holding on to the breaking branch for grim life. He is in much pain, and his grip is getting weaker. He looks down, and all he sees is a huge precipice. Suddenly he hears a voice from heaven; it is God saying, "I am here for you, all you have to do is let go and I will grab you and lift you up out of this predicament, I will protect you and put you on the right path."

The guy thinks about it for a second and says, "Is there anybody else up there?"

It is hard to let go when we are used to doing everything in our own strength, but our strength is limited, and never lasts. Our emotional muscles get tired, and we eventually fall into the abyss of our damage. All our capacities and strengths at the end of the day are lost.

Holding onto God and letting God hold on to us causes us to tap into His wonderful resources of His wellspring of life. We then start to muscle up into the character of Christ.

A good example of this character is His Joy. His joy will always fill the gap.

What is important to remember is that joy is not a feeling such as happiness. I remember saying to my son when he was feeling anxious, "feelings are like clouds they come and they go, but the sun remains the same".

Joy is a state of being. Joy does not rely on circumstances or emotional highs. Joy is a constant state of being and is not produced by everything going ok, nor is it affected by success or the lack thereof.

Joy is the fruit of the presence of God coming out of our spirit and being released from our soul into the world around us. Joy, being a fruit of the Spirit, helps fill the void. This void once filled becomes the proverbial spiritual fruit bowl for life.

Joy, as in all the fruit of the Spirit, has an overflow affect that fills us constantly where we are so satisfied with the fuel of joy that we can pass it on to others like a beautiful flowing cascade. This cascade refreshes and waters tired souls. This can be passed on.

We don't need to get any counterfeit resources for our highs from our limited resources anymore, such as performance traps, partying, and self-serving relationships for a happiness fix. The state of joy eclipses such feelings as we stay stedfast in our vertical position.

The fruit of the Spirit ministers to people in their hurt and damaged hearts. These spiritual fruit seeds can get planted in those damaged hearts and, in the right environment and timing through love and prayer, can germinate into a supernatural harvest that can be passed on and shared by all.

Praise God for His super abundant capacity of joy that is so available and can be released to each of us for the asking.

Peace

Peace is a fruit of the Spirit that comes through prayer and thanksgiving.

God's word in (Philippians 4:6-7) says, "Be anxious for nothing, but in everything by prayer and supplication, with thanksgiving, let your requests be made known to God; and the peace of God, which surpasses all understanding, will guard your hearts and minds through Christ Jesus."

It is also good to remember that Jesus is the "Prince of Peace" (Isaiah 9:6-7).

Another great breakthrough revelation that came to me was the realization, 'THAT IN CHRIST IT IS NOT ME PERFORMING IN GOD, BUT IT IS GOD PERFORMING IN ME'.

This reality brought me to the understanding of 'THE WE POSITION' (Galatians 2:20), "It's no longer I who live but Christ lives in me." This reality brought me into the position of constantly saying to my heavenly business partner,

VERTICAL LIVING

"What are **we** doing now?"

So, there you have it, but of course, it comes with a qualified caveat. That is God's command, "Be anxious for nothing, but by prayer and supplication, with thanksgiving." Then the peace comes to us.

There is a necessity of manouvering in the Prince and the Princess position, to live in the vertical.

We need to constantly reposition and recalibrate, and gauge our situation and relationship with God through mindfulness and prayer throughout the day.

It is important to remember that just like storms move, we need to stay mindful and proactive to stay in the eye of the storm. That is where it is calm and safe.

The same can be said for the attitudenal and spiritual storms of life. Our mindfulness is necessary and needs to be combined with dedication and discipline of heart to guage and change our attitudenal positioning to stay in God's will and purpose. Every time we are mindful of God and communicate with Him, we are in prayer. It only takes a moment to separate yourself from our natural egocentric reality and go to the supernatural realm in the vertical and say, **"BUT WHAT DO YOU SAY, LORD?"**

As we dedicate to the vertical through the 'love, joy, peace, patience, if not why not' gauge, we are practicing living in the moment.

We then reposition ourselves back into the centre of the eye of the storm into God's peace.

Anxiety, by nature, is a symptom from being bound and caught up in the vortex of some trauma of the past or the fear of the 'what if's' in our future. This positioning stifles our peace in the present and hinders us from moving forward into our God Blessed future.

IDENTITY

THANKSGIVING, THE KEY TO PEACE

We are not thanking God for the circumstances. Instead, we move into thanksgiving because He is with us in the circumstance. Letting our "requests to be made known", means to pray specifically, letting God know your needs and releasing them to Him through that spirit of thanksgiving moves us through the doorway into God's peace.

Thanksgiving is also designated in scripture as 'a sacrifice of praise'. Hebrews 13:15 says, "Therefore by Him let us continually offer the sacrifice of praise to God, that is, the fruit of our lips, giving thanks to His name." So as stated in this scripture, a sacrifice of praise, which is also termed thanksgiving, moves us into peace.

So, the principle of thanksgiving is that you don't say thanks because of the situation you are in. You give thanks because God is with you in it and will help you get through it.

Resetting ourselves in the vertical helps us get back to the reality of the moment and to discern if we are functioning in our proper design and full potential. It allows us to maneuver and position ourselves to be in the 'eye of the storm'.

'THE EYE OF THE STORM'.

The storms of life are ongoing because of the nature of spiritual warfare. If you think of these storms like a tropical cyclone, hurricane, or tornado, they are all similar in respect of having an eye, i.e., the eye of the storm.

In the eye of the storm, there is peace, stillness and a sense of tranquility. Even though close by, there is the vortex of destruction.

As we maintain our vertical positioning, we are maneuvering ourselves so that we don't get caught up in the horizontal emotional and mindset vortexes of life, where the enemy can rip you off. In this situation, the enemy can do ongoing damage and keep you away from your peace and stillness. You are led away from the 'vertical', the eye of the storm. You are then literally sucked in, into the vortex of destruction - in the horizontal, this is the enemy's territory.

God's word says, "Be still and know that I am God" (Psalm 46:10), and this is how we position ourselves to stay in His peace. As we position ourselves in His presence, it takes us to a place beyond human understanding where we can emerse ourselves. It's like having a spiritual shower. **(Acts 3:19) says, "Repent therefore and be converted, that your sins may be blotted out, so that times of <u>refreshing</u> may come from the presence of the Lord."**

As we continually reposition and reset ourselves in a state of repentance, which is really being able to say sorry. we not only have His peace, but we are also spiritually refreshed. This situation allows us to carry on strong, for the 'long haul'.

It is like pacing yourself in a marathon. In a marathon, a good athlete can pick up on his signals of fatigue. The athlete will then adjust his pace to cover himself from getting overly tired. Under this mindful covering, the athlete feels refreshed. (Hebrews 12:1) "Let us run with endurance, the race set before us."

This Godly mindfulness and covering is a place of ongoing protection because we are covered under the "shadow of His wings." (Psalm 91:1), "He who dwells in the secret place of the Most High Shall abide under the shadow of the Almighty."

In the book of Mark 4:37-39 scripture speaks of Jesus being asleep in a boat with His disciples. A terrible storm arose. The disciples woke Jesus up and said, "do you not care that we are perishing"? Jesus spoke to the storm and said, "peace be still", then there was a 'great calm'.

He said to the disciples, "why are you fearful, how is it that you have no faith".

IDENTITY

Just as Jesus was with the disciples and spoke peace into the stormy environment, so we in His authority can speak into our stormy environments.

As we also are in this boat of life in many stormy seas, know that our hearts and minds are also protected through faith in this vertical position of His love.

As the scripture says, we are in Christ Jesus and under His covering, no matter what the situation. This is the PEACE we have in Christ; you can't be more protected than that.

PATIENCE

Now patience is a state of our will. Jesus said, "Your will be done on earth as it is in heaven."

Patience is the fruit that comes from our choice to submit our will to God's greater purpose.

God's will would also include God's timing. There are things at play in our life that have Kingdom purposes. These purposes are way beyond our understanding and reasoning and are determined by God's timing and purpose.

In Jeremiah 29:11 scripture says, "For I know the thoughts that I think toward you," says the Lord, "thoughts of peace and not of evil, to give you a future and a hope." The word 'thoughts' can also mean 'plans'.

Can you remember the long car trips as children or even later with your own children, and saying, "Are we there yet"? Of course, the return answer was, "We will get there when we get there!" The children would eventually calm down and accept the reality of time and purpose, and we would soon arrive at the destination.

The essence of 'patience is choosing and accepting God's perfect timing, plan, and purpose as being the right one. Then agreeing with His time plan, and purpose over your life.

It is like you're on a journey going into unchartered territory. But the good news is that you have this amazing, experienced, trustworthy guide who knows the way and is guiding us along the way.

The Holy Spirit knows when there needs to be directional change and when to initiate that change and why. Only God's order can bring us into the perfect aligning of events so that His Kingdom's purposes, which are for our best interest, can be attained.

There are two essential elements to patience, one is trust and the other is the submission of your will to that greater plan and purpose which is beyond our understanding.

Scripture speaks of this, in

Isaiah 55:8-9, "For My thoughts are not your thoughts, nor are your ways My ways," says the Lord. "For as the heavens are higher than the earth, so are My ways higher than your ways, And My thoughts than your thoughts."

When you choose to trust, you can submit your will into the better ways, purposes and timing. By its very nature, our will needs to be regularly recalibrated like a compass in the journey of life. I think a very good question to put to our guide and friend, Jesus and His Holy Spirit, is, **"What are we doing now?"** Another good question is, **"But what do you say"?**

In this, we will continue to follow and trust in the direction we are going and the timing. It will cause us to move into the Godly fruit of **PATIENCE.**

TO EVERYTHING THERE IS A SEASON AND A TIME FOR EVERY PURPOSE UNDER HEAVEN (Eccl 3:1)

One of the most significant areas of amazement in my life is contemplating the exact timing of events that changes lives and destinies. Then, you think about the chances of such timing and the mutual events that had to occur for this circumstance to fall in place for a specific life-changing event to happen.

IDENTITY

A good example could be the timing of how and when you met your future spouse? You realize it is like trying to get a handle on space and the universe - it's so mind-boggling and so much bigger than us. I remember vividly a myriad of different circumstances coming together for good friends of mine and their extended family.

1/ My friend had this strong sense of renovating a part of his house and turn it into a flat. He had a real sense of urgency.
2/ This friend's sister and brother-in-law had been given notice to vacate their rental. At the same time, a neighbor next door to my friend was moving overseas and was going to AirBnB his house. So, my friend encouraged his neighbor to rent the house out for twelve months to his sister and brother-in-law.
3/ The friend's mother met a couple from New Zealand. At the same time, this couple had a daughter who wanted to study in Sydney and needed a flat.
    As this was happening my friend had just finished his renovations., After a few different options, the young girl felt at peace about renting out my friend's flat, which was only just ready to have a tenant.
4/ This young girl then meets the new neighbors who had just moved in next door.
5/ She meets the son of the new neighbours. A romance ensues, and within eighteen months, they are married and living in New Zealand. Woah.

The point being - God's plans and purposes and timing is perfect and so far beyond our comprehension. So why are we worrying? Just keep trusting, stepping out in faith, and celebrate that God has it sorted. Impatience generally comes from our will wanting to be in control of our destiny and purpose.

As our willfulness makes us impatient, so our willfulness can make us patient. As Jesus said, "Your will be done on earth as it is in heaven." As we choose God's will and purpose for our lives every day and ask for the Holy Spirit to continually be our trusting guide, we will grow in all the fruit of the Spirit.

Fruit grows through watering the proverbial plant of faith. We are watered by the word. Ephesians 5:26 says, "That He might sanctify and cleanse her with the washing of water by the word. " So remember to have your daily spiritual shower with the word of God.

The more we believe, the more we grow in faith. "Faith comes by hearing and hearing by the word of God" (Romans 10:17). By reading and believing in God's word, the more our fruit grows, especially patience. So, don't stop the watering and being watered. If we do stop we only get dried out, brittle and we will be more likely to break under the strain of impatience. So, let's stick to the better virtue of PATIENCE.

CHAPTER 3

Relationships

The first chapter of this book speaks of our design. The second chapter tells of our identity. This chapter speaks of the necessity of building and maintaining the structural integrity of relationships.

Any solid and secure structure must, by principle, be built on strong foundations.

Any sound engineer knows that they must apply universal principles based on the law of physics. Then, they can have full confidence in what they are building, knowing that the structure will be strong, safe, and supportive of life in all its many expressions.

Many forces can come against such structures, such as gravity, pressures of the earth, wind pressures, heat influences etc. Anything being built up, including us, must be governed by foundational empirical principles. Without these principles, eventually, everything will come crashing down under the pressures of life, including relationships.

In the science of physics there is the 'law of thermodynamics. One of these laws states, 'That all systems left to themselves are designed to degenerate and breakdown.' You could say that this principle is the same for us, if we are left to ourselves in relationships.

Therefore, it is only through the supernatural, miraculous power of God in Jesus Christ that we can stay strong, endure and overcome the forces of this world that would want to break us down in our relationships. The quality of these foundational principles and their implementation must start in the home.

As we stick to the foundational principles of the vertical and vertical living, we can truly be victorious, in our family unit and in society.

THE ONE FLESH PRINCIPLE

First and foremost, the principle bedrock for this relational foundation is between a husband and a wife. As Jesus said in Mark 10 :6-9 "But from the beginning of the creation, God 'made them male and female.' 'For this reason, a man shall leave his father and mother and be joined to his wife, and the two shall become one flesh'; so, then they are no longer two, but one flesh. Therefore, what God has joined together, let not man separate."

SACRIFICIAL LOVE

The basis for this bedrock belief on which such a relational structure can grow strong and stable under all pressures is, sacrificial love. It is the love that was not only expressed, carried out, and fulfilled by Jesus but He also imparted His love to us as our life resource through the power of His Holy Spirit.

Our relational integrity in this life can only start with our relationship with Jesus. Anything other than His love resource for us is counterfeit and will lead to relational breakdown because it is the wrong fuel.

God's love fuel empowers this 'love vehicle', us, to move forwards to go onwards and upwards in growing relational integrity.God, In His love, through His love, and for His love, has a wonderful destination

RELATIONSHIPS

for each one of us. The sacrificial love of Jesus will empower us to be victorious over all situations. It will also be the source and resource for the people who we connect with in our lives. In the belief that we are by design, spirit, soul and body, it is understandable that the pressures formed against us will affect us in like form.

On a spiritual level, there are demonic forces that are against all relationships. These forces will do whatever they can to disrupt and break down our relational integrity. This is done through the flesh nature of man, which is in enmity, i.e., the enemy, at war, (Romans 8:5-7) with our spirit and with God.

If our thinking, through our 'heart compass' goes to our flesh nature, it will always err to selfish thinking and self-gratification. It causes us to honor ourselves first and not our partnership with God or our partnership in our marriage.

This situation allows the spiritual enemy to come into the door of our relational household. It then starts to break down the spiritual mortar of sacrificial love. It is this mortar that holds our relational integrity together. Without this mortar, relationships will crumble.

As this integrity breaks down, we begin to think of ourselves and our needs first, rather than our partner. We then start to break down the mortar of God's word, which says in Ephesians 5:25, "Husbands love your wives, just as Christ also loved the church and gave Himself for her".

This is the essence of sacrificial love. To choose and act on serving the other person's needs over your own.

It doesn't mean being a slave or a doormat, as scripture says in Mathew 22:37, "To love your neighbor as yourself." In this there needs to be a balance. We need to be mindful of our love and integrity to and for ourselves as well and to seek God's will in whatever situation we are in.

We can do this by going back to God and asking for His direction and His purpose for us in any given situation. The verse before this is to love God first. This would suggest that in all things, get fueled up with God's love first and then with your heart compass, get God's lead, second. To do this, we need to put our agendas on the altar of love, which means to die to our own desires first and get God's desires in the forefront of our minds.

A good question, which helps us get back to the vertical, is to say, 'But what do you say Lord'? We then tap into the right fuel resource according to our design instructions.

Our fuel and resource for growing and maintaining our spiritual household must and can only be tapped into through the love of Jesus Christ and His imparting gift given to us His Holy Spirit. Only then can we move in His authority and empowering grace to overpower all evil intent trying to destroy our family unit and our society.

If this principle is not in place, our spirit starts to be ruled by our soulish desires, where our mind, will, and emotions take over. This then blocks our spiritual authority, taints our pure fuel resource, and damages the internal workings of our design. We then start to live out of our feelings and not faith. This is the nature of 'horizontal living'.

"DON'T LIVE LIFE BY HOW YOU FEEL, LIVE LIFE BY HOW YOU FEEL LED"

One of my little sayings is, "Don't live by how you feel but live by how you feel led." It comes into being by putting your will on the 'altar of love'. As Jesus said, "Your will be done", then follow Joshua's example and say to God, "What does my Lord say to His servant?" Joshua (5:14) or colloquially, "What do you say, Lord?" This moves us back into the vertical.

We must choose every day who we will serve and honor. "Choose this day whom you will serve" (Joshua 24:15). So, it is up to us to choose, continually through the day, who to serve, God or self.

The good news is that as we choose the vertical in our relationship with God and others, we create a habit pattern. It allows our spiritual muscle of serving and honoring God first, to get stronger over time, and our first 'go to', rather than to our flesh nature.

To maintain good discipline, we need to be strategic. On a physiological level, it takes three months to change habits. This change relates to actual brain cell transformation. It takes approximately one month to create new habits and three months for brain cell break down, to get rid of old bad habits.

When it comes to changing habits we tend at times to give up too soon.

SET YOUR TIMER ON THE HOUR FOR THREE MONTHS

A good strategy in practicing right relational thinking is to set up a timer on your mobile and for it to go off on the hour. You then do a thirty-second reset to check your attitude - keep doing this exercise for three months.

Remember your checklist, 'love, joy, peace, patience. If not, why not'? This simple strategy helps you to keep short accounts - it will help you align your heart with the heart of God. Your agenda is then with God's agenda, this releases yourself into His will for you and your family.

Concerning relationships, there is an order of service.

God's word says, "cast your cares upon me "(1Peter 5:7)

It is this positioning like using your God compass that brings in the right order and direction in dealing with your feelings.

You see, feelings are a very important part of life - they can be a very helpful barometer of our environment, whether it is safe or hostile. Feelings can promote many different hormone responses in the body, such as endorphins, serotonins, dopamine. There are other opposing hormones such as adrenalin, noradrenalins, kinins, cortisol's, etc.

But, with good foundations, there is a natural and a supernatural order to how this life should be lived. The order is 1/ loving God first. 2/ loving ourselves with and through His love and 3/ loving our neighbor, that includes our spouse as ourselves.

This order empowers us to be a 'love resource' for everybody else. Where we don't run down, get depressed, or burn out, and we don't look for greener pastures, which don't exist as 'the grass is only greener where you water it.'

Jesus said, in John 7:38, "He who believes in Me," as the Scripture has said, "Out of his heart will flow rivers of living water."

When we tap into His resources, His love flows into us and then out of us. We then can function to our full capacity and potential in God, and it empowers us to empower others, especially our families. If this doesn't happen, we then use our own resources where the stress of daily life starts to build up toxic side effects in us and on all our three levels of being, spirit, soul, and body.

Going to 'the vertical' allows us to cast our cares and concerns upon Jesus. The longer we try to sort everything out of our individual flesh resources, we will short circuit very quickly. We are designed to tap into the generator of life and stay powered up. Instead, our self-serving battery resource depletes very quickly, and short circuiting begins.

Serving our self becomes 'self-gratification'. Our resource then comes from pride, ego, prestige, power, possessions, entertainment, the lusts of life, and many more. They become self-serving idols in our life. They will satisfy for a very short time, but like taking drugs, we always want more, which eventually harms us. They are a bad substitute that will never satisfy.

If we live out of our feelings as our foundation for living, these feelings will become toxic and infiltrate our entire being and our relationships.

We start to live out of the pains and griefs of life with all their symptoms of anger, resentment, jealousy, bitterness, unforgiveness, hatred, and self-hatred all the way to murder, which generally is shown more through attitudinal agendas. But as we know, the side effects of these attitudes can be fully felt and expressed physically in our bodies. It can show in the form of many medical conditions and diseases if we allow these feelings to fester into a toxic lifestyle.

I remember a sad time when my cousin at the age of twenty-three died from an asthma attack while he was playing football.

He was married but had no children.

We went to his funeral. Throughout the day I was trying to work out and analyse how I would feel and how I would I cope if it was my spouse that had died.

I suppose I was trying to somehow prepare myself for such a possible event.

Thinking on these things at the end of the day I went to bed. The next morning, I woke up and went to get out of bed. My neck suddenly locked up in pain. I couldn't move my head for five days.

Through going through this painful neck experience, I realized that loss and grief is a part of life for all of us.

We can't prepare for these times of pain and grief.

What we can do is this, we can cast our cares, our grief, our pains and sorrows over to God as we try to cope with the flood of pain and trauma that goes with this life.

His comforting Grace becomes our healing buffer in our times of grief and loss. Scipture says; Isaiah 53:4-5

[4] Surely, He has borne our griefs and carried our sorrows; Yet we esteemed Him stricken, smitten by God, and afflicted. [5] But He was wounded for our transgressions, He was bruised for our iniquities, the chastisement for our peace was upon Him, And by His stripes we are healed.

We can't escape from the pains of life, but we can trust that Jesus has already taken all that we could possibly go through.

Jesus has already partnered us in all our pains and griefs, as we choose to partner him and hand over whatever we are going through we then are able to receive his healing Grace which will carry us through the traumas of life.

IF YOU CAN'T EAT RESTFULLY, DON'T EAT

Another example of the physical relationship and consequence of stress is eating a meal when you are not relaxed. It will soon lead to indigestion due to the lack of proper blood flow. Under any form of negative stress, the body is in fight or flight mode, so our blood supply has gone to the limbs for defense.

Eating under stress will eventually lead to inflammation and damage.

The same can be said for the negative communication in relationships.

A good rule of thumb for good digestion is - If you can't eat in a restful and relaxed state, then don't eat at all. Please wait for the right time, which is when you can eat restfully. Your sympathetic nervous system can take a well- earned rest. You then can give your parasympathetic nervous system a proper chance to do it's job. Then your digestion and assimilation will not be hindered, your body will be much happier and so will you.

This same rule should be applied to protecting relationships. In other words, don't speak in a reactive way in the heat of the moment.

Take time out, let the flow of love return and speak from the place of mutual respect.

REPENTANCE AND FORGIVENESS IS THE CIRCUIT BREAKER FOR OUR DESIGN BREAKDOWN

In parenting, when we tap into Jesus' love base, His love will create an atmosphere of relational confidence and security, which is then received and outworked into the hearts of the children.

In this day and age, we truly need to ask for God's help. The degree of destruction of the family unit shows in a glaring way through the break down in societal values and Godly standards.

In our human nature, we can push and force to turn life around to suit ourselves, but it is like trying to turn a ship without a rudder. There is a prophetic standard that we need to pray in. "My strength is made perfect in weakness." We need to have a faith rudder in place, or we will keep going around in relational circles wondering why we're not moving forwards in our relationships.

There are so many delinquents (men children) out there, who have not been able to fully grow up. They want their wives to cover and protect them rather than the man being the covering. In like manner women can become hard and brittle and move away from respect.

"He who dwells in the secret place of the Most High. Shall abide under the shadow of the Almighty. I will say of the LORD, "He is my refuge and my fortress; My God, in Him I will trust" (Psalms 91:1-2).

This is our rightful position, to place ourselves under God's covering, then we are properly covered. If we choose not to be under God's covering, it will be like a plant without moisture being under the sun's harsh rays.

Your family unit will wither and become brittle due to the lack of covering and protection. This makes the destruction of that family unit more probable, as statistics show.

If we stay in our damage, we remain damaged. It is only through repentance between you and God, forgiving and being forgiven, that you can move back under God's covering. Then His healing grace will manifest in you and through you and into the family.

We need the 'Father Heart of God' to empower us. There Is a strong prophetic judgment on all of us for this day and age. It comes from (Malachi 4:5-6) -

"Behold, I will send you Elijah the prophet Before the coming of the great and dreadful day of the Lord. And he will turn the hearts of the fathers to the children, And the hearts of the children to their fathers, lest I come and strike the earth with a curse."

For the sake of our families and the generations to come, we need to cry out to God to be set free from sin. This will happen through daily repentance. As I mentioned before, think of it as having a daily shower and soap up with the fragrance of Christ and smell the difference.

As you read these words it would be a good time to present or represent yourself before God.

Find a quiet place and say out loud,

"Heavenly Father, thank you for your love. Create in me a clean heart and renew the right spirit within me. Thank you, Heavenly Father, for giving me your Son, the Lord Jesus Christ. Lord Jesus, I thank you for dying for my sins. You were resurrected on the third day to give me your eternal life. I confess that you are God the Son.

Lord Jesus, I receive you into my heart as my Lord and Saviour. Heavenly Father, in Jesus' name, forgive me for all my sins. Thank you, Heavenly Father, for I am now forgiven. I am now counted as a son or daughter in Christ Jesus. Heavenly Father fill me now with your Holy Spirit and help me that I may serve you and honor you through the power of your Holy Spirit, from this day and forever, in Jesus Name Amen."

Forgiving ourselves and each other is an essential component of this sacrificial love. This leads to the growth and integrity of the family unit, which in turn grows a strong and healthy society.

1 Peter 2:5 says, "You also, as living stones, are being built up a spiritual house, a holy priesthood, to offer up spiritual sacrifices acceptable to God through Jesus Christ."

Our capacity to honor that position can only be achieved through sacrificial love. It reminds me of a song, 'Love Hurts'. It hurts because our flesh nature must die for the sake of serving and honoring somebody else other than ourselves.

As I have said earlier, the essence of being a good soldier is to honor your commander and be dead to yourself for the sake of your commission. In 1 Corinthians 15:31 God's word says, "I die daily." Civilians, by nature, will run away from danger. But a soldier's mentality will move forward to take on the task at hand, and be obedient to the commander's orders, even unto death. This is the soldiers honor and duty.

Romans 6:11 states, "Likewise, you also, reckon yourselves to be dead indeed to sin, but alive to God in Christ Jesus our Lord."

1 Corithians 6:19-20 states, "Our lives are not our own, we were bought at a price, and you are not your own, for you were bought at a price; therefore, glorify God in your body and in your spirit, which are God's."

It is a clear direction and command of God. Every day we need to actively choose, 'make your choice,' to keep your soldier's uniform on, then choose who you are going to serve and honor today. Then as a good soldier, act on the command of God.

Then watch God, through your actions, 'do great things.'

WHAT IS YOUR SECRET?

It was asked of me once by a youth pastor who had some young children of his own. He said, "What is your secret"? He knew my three children who were in their late teens at the time. His question to me was regarding how we brought up our children. I was pondering his question, saying to myself and asking God all at the same time, "What is the secret?" Suddenly the answer came to me in a flash.

I answered and said, "It's how I treat my wife!" The grace that empowers us to love our spouses sacrificially trickles into the hearts of our children as they recognize this love expressed by their parents. This ongoing parental example produces a foundational base of confidence and grace in our children.

This blessing can be past on generationally.

It can only be through the love of Jesus that we can genuinely love sacrificially and continue to submit to each other in His love (1Peter 5:5) over a lifetime.

It is His empowering Grace that gives us the capacity to live a lifestyle of 'submitting to one another in love' (Ephesians 5:21). It is then up to us to daily go to 'the vertical' and tap into that Grace resource.

Again, 'the grass is still greener wherever you water it'.

Any good gardener knows that if you have a plant that grows wonderful fruit, it is the gardener's responsibility to nurture that plant. You keep the grubs away from your beautiful plant, you take out the weeds and continually water your plant, knowing that through your efforts the plant grows beautifully with strong roots. The gardener is confident that the fruit will come and more beautiful plants will be produced.

These same principles must be applied to growing a family – In being rooted in His love we will see the growth of strong and prosperous families which in turn produces a strong society.

Unfortunately, because our society has moved away from Godly principles, evil grubs have entered our government and our society, allowing Godless laws into our community and educational systems. God's truth is paraded as lies and lies are shouted out as truth.

Our media flaunts and normalizes all sorts of lusts into our lounge rooms, where ungodly leftist belief systems have taken over parental control. Where basic discipline and boundaries in how we bring up our children is frowned against and even legislated against.

It is these 'powers and principalities (Ephesians 6:12-20) of this age that are the grubs that have infiltrated the plant of our family unit. This is leading to the plant being eaten up and destroyed from within, in our families and society. This is the reality of spiritual warfare being waged against us.

This quotation is true today as in the past. "The only thing necessary for the triumph of evil, is for good men to do nothing."

What do you say? Do not allow the plant of your family to get brittle, wither and die. Fight for the health and the wellbeing of your marriage, your family, and your society. It starts with you, in the home, here and now. (Matthew 4:17) "Repent for the Kingdom of Heaven is at hand.

CHAPTER 4

The Journey - Smell The Roses Along The Way

When God created man, He created man in His image and likeness. God has always been a God of relationship. His desire has always been to commune, chat, discuss, and relate with us, His children. His passion is also for each one of us to have the same desire for a relational intimacy and a wish to commune with Him.

From the beginning in Genesis 3:8 God's desire was to walk with His children and commune with them in the garden of Eden, in the cool of the day. God's desire for us is still the same today.

When Jesus first appeared in His resurrected body, it was to meet with His disciples in the new covenant relationship. Jesus also wants to meet with us in this journey of love and faith. He also wants to be our friend. Jesus said, "I call you friends" (John 15:15).

As in the earlier discussion on the disciples journeying to Emmaus, they, at the end of this journey, asked Jesus to 'abide', i.e., to stay with them. Jesus did. He broke bread with them and communed with them, and then He vanished.

Suddenly, their eyes were opened, and they knew Him. They discovered that it was Jesus who was with them, giving them insight and understanding of Himself and revealing their purposes In Him. They said, "Did not our heart burn within us while He talked with us on the road" (Luke 24:32).

I believe God wants us to have that same experience and revelation of His love and His plans and purposes for us along the whole journey of our life and not just at the end of it. So often, we are blinded by our own griefs, pains, and sorrows. It is only in giving them to our companion and friend Jesus that we can truly be free and are more able to recognize that Jesus is with us in the journey.

There are many times in our journey when Jesus, through His Holy Spirit, is talking to us. I pray that we can all become more sensitive and discerning of our friend's still small voice.

As princes and princesses of the kingdom, nothing we can do, good or bad, can change our position and relationship with God. "Nothing can separate us from the love of God" (Romans 8:39). Prayer becomes supernaturally natural as we walk and talk daily with our Lord and friend.

God has not changed. He still wants to walk with us through the garden of our life, for us to enjoy Him and for Him to enjoy us. So, let's walk in the garden of life with Him and smell the roses along the way.

AS PRINCES AND PRINCESSES WE WALK THIS JOURNEY OUT OF OUR OK-NESS NOT FOR OUR OK-NESS

This means that when we are sons and daughters as well as being friends with God, we don't have to prove ourselves. We can relax and enjoy our walk of love and friendship. Our reality becomes all about enjoying each step, walking out our journey of life with Him, through Him, and for Him. Knowing that Jesus is always with us and for us. It is not even about us working in God, but about God working in us.

The Holy Spirit will show us and lead us every day. We will step out in faith as God puts desires in our hearts as we are led by His love, joy, peace and patience. His word says, "I will never leave you nor forsake you" (Hebrews 13:5).

As we grow more and more in the understanding and revelation of God's love for us, we are more able to let His purposes and plans work in us and through us and will influence many lives. So, our life becomes not about I or me, but always about 'WE'.

IT DOESN'T MATTER WHAT'S AROUND THE CORNER, GOD IS ALREADY THERE PREPARING THE WAY

I had a poster once. The poster was a photograph of a beautiful garden with a pathway meandering through the garden. The way the photo was designed, it was like I was walking in the garden, stopping now and then to smell the roses and look at the beautiful flowers and trees and shrubs along the way.

As I looked ahead, I could see a beautiful sun - drenched valley. Then suddenly I realized that the path I was on, did a quick 'dogleg' behind a huge hedge, I couldn't see the path anymore.

Straight away, I thought to myself, "I wonder what's behind the hedge?" I then noticed that there was a caption in the bottom right-hand corner of the photo, it read**: -**

> **It doesn't matter what is around the corner for God is already there preparing the way.**

Straight away, I thought, "Gotcha!" But, more than this, I realized that even though I was not concerned about what was ahead around the corner behind the hedge, I realized that I had stopped enjoying all those beautiful moments along the way. I had stopped communing with my friend Jesus. I thought to myself, what a waste.

It is the same with our journey walking in the garden of life. What a waste of time and energy constantly worrying or concerning ourselves with what is ahead of us, 'what's around the corner? 'The what if' syndrome. Especially when we have Jesus with us, walking the journey with us. When you look at it, it seems so dishonoring and disrespectful of our friendship and love base with our Lord and Saviour. What do you think?

CHAPTER 5

This Moment

I remember a movie called 'City Slickers'. In this movie, one of the characters was going through the stress of what is called a 'midlife crisis'. This condition happens when people feel that everything that they have done and achieved in their life has come to an end. As a result, they lose their sense of direction and their own identity and do not know what to do next. People in this predicament feel somehow stifled or blocked; they feel a bit stuck. They are unsure about how to move forwards.

This character in the movie decides to become a cowboy on a cattle drive. And through this experience he tries to find himself. In this movie this character looks up to this rugged old cowboy, who he respects as a mentor and a father figure. The old cowboy gives this character some advice, a life principle. The rugged old cowboy says to him in a cowboy drawl, "Do you know what the most important thing in life is?"

The lost character says, "No, what is it?"

The old cowboy lifts his index finger up and says, "This."

The lost character looks incredulously at the cowboy's lifted-up index finger and asks, "What does that mean?"

The old cowboy says, "Well, that is for you to find out!"

Of course, the point is that we all need to find out for ourselves what is the most important thing in life.

I went up to my three children and I asked them the same question, "What is the most important thing in life"?

Of course, they asked, "What?"

I answered by also lifting my index finger up and saying, "This!"- showing my index finger, then I continued by saying, "This moment in God."

I quickly asked them a second question, and said,

"What is the next most important thing in life?" And again, they said, "What?" I lifted my index finger again and said, "This moment in God."

This moment is all we have until the next moment. Each moment could be our last breath. What are we going to do with this moment in time? Is it in God or not, we need to 'choose' (Joshua 24:15)?

In each moment it doesn't matter the size or the space between the four walls that surround you. All that matters is whether you are comfortable in your skin or not. Everything else is just a picture.

Is your moment, right now, in God or not? With God or without? For God or yourself? Each moment is your choice to be empowered or disempowered. To be in faith or out of faith. To trust or not to trust. To live from a base of fear or to live from a base of love.

Here is a line from another movie 'Troy' - "Take it, it's yours." This moment!

CHAPTER 6

Shut Up And Keep Kicking

My family and I were on holiday at a lovely Northern NSW coastal town called Southwest Rocks. We were staying with friends at a place called Smokey Cape Light House.

One afternoon we went for a surf to a deserted beach north of the lighthouse. We noticed a rocky outcrop with a lovely tidal pool about thirty meters out. You could walk out to it at low tide. So, a few of us went out. We stayed there for some time, floating in this tidal pool with the waves crashing over us. It was a beautiful sunny afternoon, so relaxing and peaceful. We were all having a great time.

Time had passed, and we realized it was time to go back to shore. What we didn't know is that the tide had changed. My son Jeremy, who was about twelve years old was with me, and we started swimming back to the shore. Jeremy and I jumped off the rock from a different place from the others.

We were about six meters from the beach, and I could feel this strong cross current hitting us and starting to take us the wrong way. Suddenly I realized that I had put my son in peril, thinking to myself, "You idiot Michael", You've put your son in danger.

What was I going to do to rescue us out of this dangerous situation? I knew I had to act quickly, and make a decision, and not panic.

I remembered the scripture, "My strength is made perfect in weakness" (2 Corinthians 12:9).

I said to God, "What should I do?" Straight away I got a vision of a surfboard. The idea was to lie on our backs and flatten our bodies out like a surfboard. This approach would cause us to get most of our body weight out of the rip by floating on the film of water, above the main force of the current.

I said to Jeremy, "I want you to float on your back and be like a surfboard and kick with your feet." This action would keep us a bit above the rip so we could make some headway and at the same time conserve some energy.

As we were kicking on our backs Jeremy looked across at me and said, "Dad, are we going to make it?"

I looked back at him and said, "SHUT UP AND KEEP KICKING!"

Interestlingly, the term "shut up" was never allowed to be used in the home as I termed it a disrespectful saying.

Ha, but in this case I deemed it necessary.

In an instant, like a 'beam me up Scotty' moment, we felt the back of our heads hit the sand, safe and sound. Jeremy got straight up and started running down the beach to play with the others. I was still lying on the beach at the water's edge, exhausted, getting over my puffing and adrenal overload!

"Shut up and keep kicking" became our family motto. So, what does this motto mean?

For me, in that moment in the rip, asking God for some direction, the answer was, whatever you have faith for, stick to it and complete the task to the end of that faith path. Never give up because of circumstances. Never give in because of what your thoughts and emotions might tell you at any given time. Don't let the fear or the 'what if's' ever distract you.

There are many ways that we can get hit by crosscurrents of life. These pressures can distract us from our focus and take us away from our calling and purpose. People will also say many things that are not coming from your faith-based position and purpose. People generally will come from their own agendas and limited preconceived ideas and attitudes.

Remember to reset your faith and say, "But what do you say, Lord?" Then wait for the faith download. Circumstances can be irrelevant to your faith position and commitment. Plus, "Without faith it is impossible to please God" (Hebrews 11:6).

Our flesh nature always wants to be in control and have a handle on everything. Faith is the reverse. It's trusting that God is in control and trusting Him in the circumstances of our own weakness. We so often fail through relying on our own strengths, which become our weaknesses.

But the word fail is really the wrong word to use. For in God we don't fail, we are merely being corrected so we can change our position and course and go in the right direction. Go God's way. God is more interested in us growing more and more into His likeness and character. Blessing us is His desire.

Romans 5:3-4, "But we also glory in tribulations, knowing that tribulation produces perseverance; and perseverance, character; and character, hope."

This hope grows, as does our character every time we call out to God in our many distresses and weaknesses. Whether it's trauma in the family - whether it's a work colleague with attitude - whether you miss out on the position of your dreams, or whether you are just fed up and exhausted. Just keep asking for more of God's love, grace and mercy; choose to trust and take your next step.

With this in mind, I think it is also crucial that we realize that when there are other people who we know and care about, who are also struggling in their weaknesses, that we ask God for discernment, so we know how or when to help them. Sometimes we can want to rescue people too soon. There are times when people need to get to the end of themselves in their own weakness so that they also cry out to God. Praying for them first and receiving God's lead is a good start. You may pray that they receive a revelational download from the Holy Spirit, or it may be praying for angelic protection, or it may be a helping hand. We all have our own journey to walk out, either with the Lord or not, so choose.

Always wait on the Lord first, rather than going off in your own mindset or emotions. Get His battle plan and strategy first.

Just like King David. David had so many 'ups and downs' in His life. But he always had the heart to seek after God's heart in all his distresses. (Acts 13:22). Reading through Psalms gives you a great example of King David continually turning to God.

God's continued grace, mercy, and forgiveness was always available for David and the same is true for us.

You step, and God moves is how faith works. You never, never know if you don't have a go. God's word says that we are to endure. (Matthew 10:22) "He who endures to the end will be saved." This is the path of growth in Christ through doing the hard yards. Just like building muscles through exercise.

As an Osteopath for close to forty years, I constantly see the value in patients staying disciplined through maintaining their exercises and postural mindfulness. I also see what happens when you stop exercising. When you stop exercising, you lose muscle within two to three weeks. Without maintaining strength, your body quickly succumbs to the stressors of life. We weaken and start to get injured.

I say to patients that life is like an escalator that is going down and we are trying to go up it. So, whatever you do, don't stop! Like a guided missile, faith takes you on a journey. The guided missile never goes straight to the mark but always moves forwards left or right through many corrections and twists and turns along the way. Every time you go left or right, you can think to yourself, "Am I going in the right direction?"

From this thought process many of us, due to our flesh nature, can start thinking negatively and become fearful of the 'what ifs'.

We can quite often balk at our positioning and change course. We so often can abandon the journey of faith and miss out on our calling. Therefore, we can choose what may be good for us, but it may not be God's best for us, and therefore never seeing or achieving our full potential.

What a shame and what a waste, simply because we moved away from the faith. This can be due to the fear of getting it wrong or being a failure or looking stupid in somebody else's eyes, who, by the way, is generally irrelevant to the situation.

(KGFI) 'KEEP GOING FOR IT'

I want to live my life to my full potential. I don't want to have one drop of my potential left in the tank. I want to use all that I was given to honor the giver of life. How about you?

I have a little acronym that I like to put down when messaging somebody as a directive and a finishing point. The acronym says, (KGFI) 'KEEP GOING FOR IT'. Never stop, never give up, keep believing and keep acting out your belief. 'Belief plus action = faith. 'KGFI' is for you too.

We need to use discretion and wisdom along the way. We are not to do this journey on our own. Jesus said, "You are my friends" (John 15:15). Think of it like this. Every step you take in this life can be a walk of faith walking along the journey with your friend Jesus. Along this walk, making the journey of life, we are not just walking - we are talking and listening to God along the way. In this, we are learning, growing and maturing in the likeness and the character of our friend.

Accept and love yourself and how God has designed you. Anything less will cause you to try and cover up your weaknesses and frailties.

God loves us and accepts us in our frailties and weaknesses, so should we. It is also imperative to realize that we are designed to be God's 'vessels of honor'. (2 Timothy 2:21). Through our availability, we become 'a vessel of honor'. God pours His love and grace into us. If we allow Him.

We are then open and available in our hearts to receive whatever God has for us. Then, as we receive His amazing grace for whatever situation is before us, we can be assured that God is doing the work in us, through our faith and obedience in God. He is always faithful.

GET OVER YOURSELF

It saves a lot of distress and moves us away from exhaustion and even sickness and emotional despair when we don't have to cover up anymore, and we don't have to try and be like somebody else. There is nobody in the whole universe like you. God says you are, "fearfully and wonderfully made" (Psalm 139:14) and that we are "the apple of His eye" (Deuteronomy 32:10).

It's time to agree with God and move into the empowering synergy of His love for you. Then you can truly love others with His love, once you start loving yourself with the love of Christ. Anything less than this positioning is disobedience and rebellion to God's word for you. Blessings and empowerment can't flow from a position of self-loathing, self-hatred and self-unforgiveness.

It is also difficult to love and forgive others if you don't love and forgive yourself. So, it is time to quit 'bad mouthing' yourself and others and come into the light of God's Love. Saying sorry and repenting should be a daily process like having that daily shower. You feel so much better.

I experienced a good example of this with myself. For many years I relied on my own pride and self-righteousness, to prove my worthiness to myself and to others. Trying to prove yourself to be good at everything can be very exhausting. This was shown to me in a dream.

THE INTRUDER AT THE DOOR

In this dream I remember that an intruder had come to my front door in the middle of the night and was going to attack my family. The following image in this dream was me walking down the stairs to take on and fight this intruder and save my family. Halfway down the stairs, it was like my whole body went to jelly, and I had no strength left in me. I was helpless and hopeless in myself.

My next thought was, "What am I going to do now?" The next image was me bowing my head to the ground and saying to God, "Lord, if you want my head to be chopped off then chop it off."

I literally got to the end of myself and my will. I had nothing left except to submit to God's will and his grace and mercy for my family and me. I also realized that my children are God's children first. I realized that He had so much more love for them and the capacity to cover and protect them than I ever could. In that same vein, He was also there for me as well.

"The battle is the Lord's" (1 Samuel 17:47). From a position of victory, we can take on all the Goliaths in our life. He battles for my children and me - He battles for you and has already won.

Whatever situation we are in, know the battle is the Lord's. Give your cares and concerns to Him, celebrate and give thanks, for He is with us in the darkest, direst moments. He will lead us through the worst-case scenarios. Trust him and stay with Him in 'the eye of the storm'.

It was time for me to move away from my willful ways and my exhaustion and choose and trust God's way.

As Jesus said, "I am the way, the truth, and the life. No one comes to the Father except through Me" (John 14:6).

It's time to stop having a 'tug of war' with God. It works much better to 'tag team' with God and is far less exhausting. It is time to stop putting yourself in a position to be swept away by the current of your feelings and your cares and concerns. It is time to start floating on the ocean of God's love and be led by the breeze of faith and hope. Then you will land on the shores of peace, joy and fulfillment.

CHAPTER 7

The Journey Of The Next Step, You Step And God Moves

'THE GETHSEMANE TWO STEP' THE DANCE OF LIFE

As in dancing, somebody must take the lead and the partner follows that lead.

In the Garden of Gethsemane (Matt 26:36) Jesus was very sorrowful and asked that He be spared from His experience to come. In His state of despair, He sought God's lead. In doing this, Jesus said, "Nevertheless, not as I will but as you will." **'The rest is history'.**

The same for us, ask for God to lead us and choose His will in the **'dance of Life'.**

'THE GETHSEMANE TWO STEP'

Our life is made up of so many moments. Making each moment a step of faith, creates a cascade of steps, where you step, and God moves. God moves you through His Holy Spirit into your destiny and the destiny of others that you meet along the way on this journey of love.

God is wooing each one of us, even when we don't know Him. What is sure, though, is that He knows each one of us. (Jeremiah 1:5) says, "Before I formed you in the womb, I knew you."

God is drawing us to himself, but there is also a condition of where our hearts are placed in this journey of life.

(2 Chronicles 16:9) says, "For the eyes of the LORD run to and fro throughout the whole earth, to show Himself strong on behalf of those whose heart is loyal to Him." Having a heart to seek after God's heart moves God into action on our behalf.

In the wrestling matches of life, it's great to know that God is your 'tag team partner'; you can't lose. These doors of life open and close as we move on in our partnership of 'faith, hope and love'" (1 Corinthians 13:13) with our Lord and Saviour.

How do we know when the time is right to step out in faith and which way to go? Do I go left or right, forwards or backwards? Where, when, and how. They are all excellent questions that become a part of our moment-by-moment reality. So, what is the answer?

"Is it time to move to the beaches"?

'Go to the word'.

After eleven years working in my first practice in Parramatta, I felt it was time to leave Parramatta and work full time from the 'Northern Beaches'.

I was driving home and asked God, "is it time to move to the beaches?

I felt led to stop the car and open up the bible and look at the first scripture I saw in the New Testament and then look at the first scripture I saw in the Old Testament.

This must of been a one off lead by the Holy Spirit because I don't think I've done it since and that was over twenty years ago.

Anyway, in faith I gave it a go.

I opened up the New Testament and my eyes went straight to (Matthew 1:22), which read, They shall call His name Immanuel, "God with Us".

I thought to myself, that's a good start.

I then went to the Old testament, remembering the question that I put to God was "Is it time to move to the beaches"?

My eye's went straight to a verse in The book of (Genesis 49:13) "Zebulun shall reside, settle down by the Haven of the sea and shall become a Haven for ships".

Wow! Praying specifically often brings with it specific miraculous answers and straight out of God's word.

The meaning was of course, that my new clinic on the Northern Beaches would be a Haven for many people that struggle with the storms of life and pain. That my clinic would be a safe harbour for them.

So I believe God loves us praying, asking and believing for specific answers.

I certainly got mine and I am still ministering in my clinical haven on the Northern Beaches today.

THE COMPASS OF PEACE AND JOY

As we seek after life and seek after truth, I believe that the Holy Spirit meets us at that point. Jesus said in John 14:6, "I am the way, the truth and the life." So, when we seek after truth and life, the Spirit of God

THE JOURNEY OF THE NEXT STEP, YOU STEP AND GOD MOVES

will manifest and influence our spirit and lead us towards His Love and enlightenment.

James 4:8 says, "Draw near to God and He will draw near to you." This can happen in overt experiences and in subtle ways, these ways may be harder to distinguish but still moves us onwards towards the mark of revelation, relationship, and freedom.

For me, I use the sense of peace and joy as my compass. Just like the compass is attracted to a magnetic influence, so are we. Either the flesh influences of this world, i.e., vain glory, power, control, all forms of self-gratification, and selfish ambitions. Or we relinquish that attraction and go to God, what I term the vertical, and say, "But what do you say, Lord?"

Choosing God's will and purpose over our own is where the proverbial 'rubber meets the road'. We then move into God's authority and empowerment. For us and all who are around us.

This repositioning of your will into God's will, where you are led by the Holy Spirit into the dance of the 'Gethsemane two step', puts you in the position of being a power pact living sacrifice. For the sake of a purpose greater than yourself. In this regard you could also say for the sake of your family.

As an Osteopath I treat many stressed out and exhausted women.

In talking with them regarding one of the causes for their painful symptoms, I will say to them, "your symptoms are caused by the 'mother syndrome'.

I explain and give them an example, the 'mother syndrome is that you may have thirty things to do every day, you get through ten and your number fifty!

Keep in mind, that you don't have to be a mother to live in the 'mother syndrome'.

In other words, they never get to look after themselves because they are too busy looking after everybody else.

Any hole that is left open will be always filled with 'stuff'.

All this stuff quite often is not the right stuff. This will lead to further dammage and exhaustion as we often fit into other peoples wants and agendas rather than what is God's best for us.

I explain to them that in that ongoing state of exhaustion that they can never be the best that they can be and will not be able to live to their full and best potential for family, friends, work, and life generally.

This reminds me of the story of Martha and her sister Mary in (Luke10:40) it says that Martha "was distracted".

i.e., fed up and exhausted from being too busy, what I would call 'over serving'.

Martha complained to Jesus that her sister Mary was at Jesus feet listening to His every word but from Martha's point of view she should have been helping her in the serving.

Jesus says to Martha, "Martha you are worried and troubled about many things, but Mary has chosen the good part".

Jesus is basically saying to all of us, get before him first and prioritize what is important. Then go where the peace takes you.

This discipline should be on a daily basis. We can get so caught up trying to fix and cover every need for everybody that we can lose sight of what is best for us and then others.

Download God's grace first for every situation for you and then others.

(2Corinthians 12:9) "My Grace is sufficient for you".

My prescription for exhausted women is to put themselves first into their daily and weekly timetable.

Once they schedule themselves in first as a priority then they can work everything else in around that priority.

It's like the inflight directive to put the oxygen mask on you first in a flight emergency. It is essential for the best outcome for everybody.

In many cases the 'mother syndrome' comes from a place of wanting to rescue others from their burdens.

But Jesus says in (Matthew 11:29-30) "take my yoke upon you". For my yoke is easy and my burden is light".

Meaning being coupled and balanced through serving Jesus. Jesus says, in this you will find "rest", a refreshing peace.

Let us go with His peace first and then the refreshing rest will follow. Then His grace will cover us in our busyness. In this we can trust him for our loved ones including ourselves.

When I was studying acting, I would work at different jobs to earn my way. In getting a job I would get a desire to try out for a particular position and if successful I would stay there until I lost the peace to remain there. If the peace left me, so would the desire, and the joy would leave me.

Even though I didn't know God at this time the principle of being led by His peace was an active element in my soul. His compass was at work in my life even though I did not know it.

For me, doing anything where there was no peace or joy would be a feeling like being in chains, enslaved to a hostile environment where I felt that I was wasting my life. To me, that was a form of being tied up and tortured.

"SORRY, I NEED TO GO" - BELIEF + ACTION = FAITH

This, of course, led me into many jobs over a short period of time - 11 jobs over 4 ½ years, to be exact. My shortest job was working in an insurance company. Here, I dismally sat behind a desk with a notebook and a calculator. There were 10 desks in front of me and then the manager's desk. After looking at these desks for 20 minutes, which I saw as 'monoliths of despair', I put my hand up and said, "Sorry, I need to go."

When I get this sense of change, it is like this weightiness comes upon me. Like a burden that doesn't lift off me until I've made a change in my direction.

Even recently, after over forty years down the track, this weightiness for change will still come upon me. I see it now as the leading of the Holy Spirit in directing my steps. Proverbs 16:9 says, "A man's heart plans his way, but the Lord directs his steps."

Recently, a friend whose offices I was using for my clinic, came into the room and mentioned that he was thinking of retiring. As he left the room, straight away, I got this 'download' in my spirit - this can be called the 'burden from the Lord' or another term is an 'unction from the Holy Spirit'. The sense or download I received was that it was time for me to move to a new location. Straight away I picked up the phone and called the senior pastor of our church, and I said, "I believe It's time we got our community center up and running."

This Centre was a vision we had talked about over the years.

He straight away said, "It's funny that you say that, as it was only last week that I was looking at new premises with that idea in mind."

I replied, "Well, I can bring my clinic onboard, if that helps." DAs were passed, renovations completed, and six months later, there I was in these new premises where the vision turned into reality, and on we go.

Asking, seeking, and knocking, (Matthew 7:7) is empowered by an attitude of belief. Acting on what we believe moves us into the supernatural relm of faith, the fourth-dimensional realm of 'the vertical'.

It is where God meets our heart's desire, and God grants the desire of our hearts. Jesus says in (John 15:7-8), "If you abide in Me, and My words abide in you, you will ask what you desire, and it shall be done for you. By this My Father is glorified, that you bear much fruit; so, you will be My disciples."

So, what does this mean as far as moving on in this journey of faith, hope, and love? This scripture speaks of 'bearing much fruit, in other words being successful in your life. This successful fruit-bearing is in seeing the essence of God's will and purpose being released in us and through us, which produces more fruit.

This action is based on choosing God's will over your own, partnering with Jesus through belief, then acting on that belief which becomes a move of faith, which God blesses. This action can only be achieved through us being qualified by abiding, i.e., staying close and dwelling in Christ, and His word abiding in us, and then being released through us.

I had a poster once, and the quote was, "Live as though Christ died yesterday, arose today, and is coming back tomorrow." So, with that thought in mind it makes every moment matter and makes every moment special as if it were your last moment. To get the sweet essence out of every drop of life we have and to give it all back to God as a living sacrifice to Him. "Which is our reasonable service" (Romans 12:1). "Being imitators of God, a sweet-smelling aroma of sacrifice" (Ephesians 5:1-2).

What is your vision? What is your goal? Scripture says, in Proverbs 29:18, "That without a vision we perish."

Ask for insight, ask for a vision, ask for direction. Believe that you will get a 'download', a sense, an unction. Then step out in faith and have a go. Remember life is a journey of the next step of faith.

'Have a go, or you'll never know'. Like that guided missile, it always makes right and left adjustments and minor corrections to get to the mark. It works the same for us.

We have a race set before us - it has boundaries and a finish line. God is our trainer; the Holy Spirit empowers us to run the good race. It's a race of endurance. So, keep running the race for your upward call and finish well. (1 Corinthians 9:24).

BE TEACHABLE IN HEART AND HUMBLE IN SPIRIT

I remember a teacher we had in primary school. His name was Mr. Roberts. He was a large red-headed man with a strong Welsh accent. He was loud and authoritative, and he didn't mind giving the cane. Nobody liked him!

I remember going home and saying to my Mum, "Nobody likes Mr Roberts." Mum said, "That must make him very sad. Why don't you look for the good in him and not the bad?"

As an twelve-year-old, I thought that was quite a novel idea. I decided to be teachable and follow my mother's wisdom. It worked! I started to see many good qualities in him. He was quite funny with a dry wit, and he was thoughtful and intelligent. He had a strong sense of order and lived by strong principles.

I got it. In no time, we became good friends. The negatives disappeared as the light of respect and acceptance took over. I still remember at one time, Mr. Roberts smiling at me and putting his hand on my shoulder and saying, "Well done."

Being teachable in heart and humble in spirit are essential qualities in the corrections of life and growing and going in the right direction. These attributes keep you flexible to change and responsive to discipline. It is also the place where we grow and mature and get transformed through the training of life. James 4:10 says, "Humble yourself in the sight of the Lord and He will lift you up." It is with the help of God's Grace covering us. Even if we do have a fall, we get up again and keep going, from strength to strength and glory to glory.

CHAPTER 8

The Bolting Horse

In making life decisions, we may not always make the right ones. I have made many wrong decisions over a lifetime - but haven't we all! It is simply a part of our human condition. So, when we do make these decisions, what do we do next?

God's word says, "And we know that all things work together for good to those who love God, to those who are the called according to His purpose" (Romans 8:28).

So, this is good news. Even when we make mistakes and get things wrong, good will come out of them, even if we don't understand why difficult events happen, and we suffer great pain, grief and hardship. But there is here a qualification in this scripture, "For those who love God." But how do we know if we love God?

First, we need to know that love is not a feeling; love is a fruit. Just as fruit grows, so does love. Therefore, just like fruit, love starts as a seed. Love begins as a seed of faith implanted into our spirit when we receive Jesus Christ into our heart as our Lord and Saviour.

For "God is Love" (1 John 4:8). We have received God's seed which is His love. As we die to ourselves and become alive in Christ, our love seed becomes buried in the soil of faith. His seed of love then germinates in us.

Consider the humble seed buried in the dark soil. It will die in that environment - this allows new life to manifest. Its internal design becomes activated into the sprouting of new life. The plant forms, which grows and matures and then produces more fruit and more seeds where life continually grows, multiplies and manifests into new life. We then become this transformed proverbial plant born out of His love.

From dying to ourselves, we become alive in Christ. "Likewise, you also, reckon yourselves to be dead indeed to sin, but alive to God in Christ Jesus our Lord"(Romans 6:11).

From this new life in us, just like the plant, we mature and grow and influence and change the landscape of life all around us. Through the ongoing death to life process, we then release more seeds of God's eternal love eternally.

We can genuinely believe for eternal kingdom purposes to bring life out of a death experience. Sometimes these experiences can be close calls as far as survival goes. At this time, thanking God for his angelic support might be in order.

Matthew 18:10 says, "Take heed that you do not despise one of these little ones, for I say to you that in heaven their angels always see the face of My Father who is in heaven."

I think for a lot of us, as His 'little ones', we have kept our angels very busy. "Thanks guys."

I remember one of my many occasions of making a wrong choice was when I was sixteen. I was walking with a friend down on the south coast in the middle of a beautiful valley. It was a sunny day, a beautiful blue sky, the sun's warmth was caressing my face, and everything seemed very peaceful.

We walked right up to these grazing horses and cows. I walked up to this one horse and patted him. He seemed quite friendly, so I took the next step minus wisdom and discernment. I decided to hold on to the horse's mane and jump on the horse, bareback of course. In an instant, the horse turned around and bolted. This bolt was no short bolt - it went on and on through this valley of my regret. I was holding on for grim life and yelling out, "woh, wohwoh!!!"

The valley floor was very rough and going past me like a blur due to the speed of the galloping horse. Falling off at breakneck speed was not an option. However, the horse was bolting at such a speed that the ride was smooth. I realized if I could hold on, my hope was that he would eventually stop. A good choice on my part, at last.

This horse did decide to stop after about a half a mile or so, down the valley and back up on the top of a lonely hill. He looked at me with a quizzical look as I slowly slid off him in a pool of cold sweat. I found out later that this horse was a paddocked racehorse long overdue for a gallop, 'lucky me'!

Life's situations can change very quickly. As in my horse-riding experience, ha-ha. In some difficult situations, holding on for grim life is the only option.

Whether a business deal has gone wrong, or a relationship is under threat due to some offence. Whether a hoped-for outcome is dashed - whatever circumstance has befallen us, sometimes we have to hold on and believe that we will get to the end of it and trust that things will work out. With every ending there is also a beginning. So, stand fast, hold the line and believe for a new day and new opportunities.

STOP! WHAT ARE YOU DOING?

In other circumstances there may be a need for a different strategy. You may realize that you are in the wrong situation or the wrong place or going down the wrong track, and you need to stop! Turn around and get the heck out of there and go back to where you need to be.

This example came to mind. It happened when we were having a lovely birthday lunch for my daughter Angie. It was held at a beach called Warriewood that is on the northern beaches of Sydney. It was a beautiful sunny day sitting down lazing back in a lovely cafe, watching the surf. We were very relaxed after finishing a delightful lunch. Then, out of the blue, my daughter and son Jeremy said, "Do you want to check out jump rock?" Jump rock is a rocky ledge on the headland at Warriewood. It is about a 13-meter drop into the ocean. A nice walk after lunch seemed like a good idea, so off we went.

On getting to jump rock and looking over the edge, the jump looked impressive and a bit of fun. But like many offers in life, it can often lead you down the slippery slope of dismay and regret.

So, in many ways a good rule of thumb is to think twice about what you say yes to.

My son and daughter then suggested that we should now walk a bit further on the path that we were on and go to 'Jump Rope'. Haha, the thing with bad decisions, they can be like slippery slopes, they can make it difficult turn back from. Jump rope is another section of the headland where you walk to another ledge and climb down a rope to get to a type of an open cave which you can swim in on a calm day. I innocently said yes, so we kept walking along the path. As we walked along the path, we loved the ocean views and enjoyed the warm breeze and the camaraderie.

Suddenly I realized that the path had diminished to 18 inches in width, flanked by a rock face on one side and a twenty-meter drop onto rocks on the other side. I realized I was now on the path of regret.My daughter said to me, "Turn around, Dad, so I can take a photo."

I came to my senses, thinking, what the heck are we doing here? I went straight into petrified shock mode and yelled out, "STOP"! What are we doing here? I'm not going any further!" My peace and joy had very quickly disappeared into the oblivion below. I slowly turned around and, carefully, taking slow, little steps, walked back to safety. My adult children kept looking quizzically at each other thinking, 'What's wrong with him?' Ha-ha. Oh, to be young again.

The moral of this story is if the inner sense of peace and joy stops, so should you. Relook at your heart compass. In a blink, ask God, "But what do you say?" If you get the sense to turn around and find a better direction, then do it. It can save a lot of pain and hardship in the long run.

The other point is always having the guts to follow your own convictions and instincts, even if other opinions may differ. What is right for somebody else may not be suitable for you. Trust in the 'still small voice', (1 Kings 19:12) the inner voice of the Holy Spirit.

FELICITY STOP!

There was another time going on my first weekend away with my girlfriend. We went with other friends to the ski fields for the June long weekend. We were within a few kilometers of our destination, and the traffic up to the mountain had stopped moving.

We all got out of the car and started playing in the snow. After a while, I went back to the car and sat on the bonnet, sitting back enjoying the warm sun on my face and watching my friends having a snow fight.

At the same time, I looked up to see the line of traffic had stopped for about one kilometer, up to the top of the hill. I also saw one lonely car driving at high speed, going the other way coming back down the hill.

I went back to watching my friends in the snow. Then, I noticed Felicity making a big snowball, she looked up at me and started laughing. She was about three meters from the roadside, and she then started running towards me with the snowball in her hand and about to run across the road.

In my mind's eye I had a quick vision like a snapshot of that car from a minute before. In an instant, I yelled out at Felicity, "Stop"! From the shock of hearing my shout, Felicity hesitated just at the side of the road as the car swerved around her at incredible speed and kept going.

Over forty years and three grown-up children later, I look at my beautiful wife, Felicity, and honestly give thanks to God that I listened to my inner voice and some possible angelic nudging. I still go into a cold sweat every time I think of that 'close call'.

PS: ever since I have always held Felicity's hand crossing roads. Ha, some memories last a lifetime.

I believe that we all need to practice, to stop, and listen to the inner voice of the Holy Spirit.

Romans 8:26-28 26. "Likewise the Spirit also helps in our weaknesses. For we do not know what we should pray for as we ought, but the Spirit Himself makes intercession for us with groanings which cannot be uttered. Now He who searches the hearts knows what the mind of the Spirit is, because He makes intercession for the saints according to the will of God. And we know that all things work together for good to those who love God, to those who are the called according to His purpose."

With this in mind, ask, seek, knock, listen, believe and act and see God's amazing Grace continue to cover, protect, empower and lead you through all the hills and valleys of this incredible life journey.

CHAPTER 9

Love Comes With Boundaries

What is a boundary? A boundary is a barrier of protection. A demarcation line which may be a verbal, attitudinal, material or a moral line that limits intrusion or influence.

The greatest boundary for life comes from the greatest commandment. The 'love boundary'. Love must come with boundaries.

The most significant boundary was the one set up by God, which was to "love God with all your heart, soul, mind and strength and to love your neighbor as yourself "(Mark 12:30-31). This love boundary puts everything else in life into the proper context and perspective. Thus, God's greatest boundary sanctifies us and empowers us for life and empowers us for everything that can come at us in life.

I liken a boundary to a water canal. A water canal is designed to capture life-giving water and protect that water, so it stays in its pure state. This water is protected from surrounding impurities. Without the protection of a water canal, the water would quickly dissipate into a muddy, putrefied mess. Unfortunately, this is exactly what happens to our own lives without moral boundaries such as "love your neighbor as yourself."

Without such values anarchy would ensue.

The water canal then provides a protective watercourse, which causes a directive flow. It leads the life-giving water to a different location where this life-giving resource will then enhance further life.

Our real-life boundaries will do the same thing. We can protect, nurture and lead each other in the way that enhances life in all its forms, attitudinally, emotionally, physically, and morally.

Unfortunately, the spirit of this age, 'the prince of this world', i.e., the spirit of the anti-Christ, has broken moral boundaries down to a form of idol worship where an individual's subjective feeling becomes of paramount importance. In this age of self-gratification, the reason and purpose for life is all about feeling good.

To maintain this idol of how I choose to feel, truths are seen as lies and lies as truth.

Romans 1:21-25 "Because, although they knew God, they did not glorify Him as God, nor were thankful, but became futile in their thoughts, and their foolish hearts were darkened. Professing to be wise, they became fools, and changed the glory of the incorruptible God into an image made like corruptible man—and birds and four-footed animals and creeping things. Therefore, God also gave them up to uncleanness, in the lusts of their hearts, to dishonor their bodies among themselves, who exchanged the truth of God for the lie and worshiped and served the creature rather than the Creator, who is blessed forever. Amen."

COMITTMENT GOVERNS FEELINGS

Now laws have been introduced to even protect an individual's feelings. This is to the point where that individual can bring charges to bear on any person by the degree to which that individual, on any given day chooses to be offended.

Ethics and moral absolutes are thrown out of the proverbial window. Godly standards are frowned upon as irrelevant in a society that thrives on moral decay based on feelings. In this place where the Godly boundaries of moral absolutes are broken down to laws based on lowest common denominator disfunctional thinking.

Society slowly breaks down and decays in a dissipated dirty mess of it's own making.

It has been the case throughout history, where civilizations rise and fall by the degree that those civilizations hold on to or break down moral and ethical boundaries.

From a Godly perspective, if we bring this water canal analogy into a life context, it would be that one side of the water canal would be to love God. The other side of the water canal would be to love your neighbor as yourself.

It is then the floor of the canal that adheres and brings integrity to the canal and makes it functional. This floor in a metaphorical sense is 'the word of God'.

God's word is the foundational floor of life that provides the principles that hold life together and protects us from our human frailties and faults. In this, our thinking doesn't get muddied, and authority and empowerment is not dissipated by double-mindedness and double standards. Where our self-centered flesh nature would lead us into a stinking quagmire of damage and regret.

Another excellent example of how boundaries are expressed in life is how parents will protect their children. Parents' verbal protection with young children can often be expressed by the term "ah ah," or "no."

If there is no positive response from the child, the boundary may be followed by a holding of the hand or a little tap on the hand. This action is to let the child know that you mean what you say and that you will back up what you say for the sake of the child's protection.

Good communication is also essential in promoting these protective boundaries for your children. So, they know they are loved through being protected.

However, in this day and age a smack on the hand or the back of the leg, is now seen as some sort of abuse. Society has brought everything down to the lowest negative common denominator, where everything is viewed and administered from the worst-case scenario position. This position is minuscule, but societies that move away from a God-based belief system, function out of fear of the future, 'the what if' syndrome and the grief of the past. This trend wants to shut down basic life principles where political ideologies try to manipulate and control the system for its own ends.

A good example of this is keeping God out of the classroom.

The overt overreach of political correctness in all its forms has come to such extremes as believing that an emotionally traumatized child can decide on what gender they want to be. The madness of this humanistic system will then say, "There, there, you're alright you can have hormones and even an operation. You can be whatever you feel you want to become."

Has the world gone diabolically nuts or what?? Talking about 'throwing the baby out with the bath water'. Which is another story in itself!

So, the very principles that protect us become the enemy of a Godless system that wants more control. Societal fear and grief that is not balanced with Godly principles, will break down the integrity of the very boundaries that protect us. Bringing back Godly boundaries enhances the health and wellbeing of our society and all relationships.

Scripture talks about us being "the head and not the tail" (Deut 28:13). In other words, we are to function in our God-given authority based on God's word for the sake of the health and well-being of our families and the community as a whole.

BECAUSE I SAID SO

One of my two most common verbals as a parent was either, "Because I love you" or "Because I said so." These two verbals promote a covering of grace and protection.

One of my greatest irritations is when I hear a parent give directions to a child, and the child doesn't obey that direction.

What compounds this rebellious spirit, which is precisely what it is, is when the parent doesn't back up their instructions to that child.

Some form of consistent discipline is so necessary to bring order, a sense of security and confidence into the life of every child. "Train up a child in the way he should go, and when he is old, he will not depart from it, (Proverbs 22:6).

The lack of proper disciplinary training says to the child that the parent's word is worthless and irrelevant. This teaches the child that, "I don't need to listen to my parents." How utterly irresponsible of the parent in the proper rearing of that child, and how disastrous can this be for the child's future. The reason being that if a child does not listen and doesn't obey a parent's instructions they could be harmed or even killed.

It is so vital and necessary that parents train their children to honor and obey the word of the parent even in minor matters, this will maintain an environment of safety, security, protection and order. My example is that if a child is not trained to be obedient and does not heed or listen to the words of the parent, what happens when they are at the edge of a roadway with busy traffic? The parent says, "Stop"! But the child has been conditioned not to listen or obey the parent's commands. The child then continues to run onto the busy roadway. The result is clear, the child is maimed or killed.

The fault lies squarely with the parent who did not train the child to honor and be obedient to the parents' word.

(EPHESIANS 6:1-3) Children obey your parents in the Lord, for this is right. "Honor your father and mother," which is the first commandment with promise. "That it may be well with you, and you may live long on the earth."

As the integrity of the water canal needs to be maintained to protect our life-giving resources, so it is with our children. In this regard, it is important that we see ourselves from the same position. That we are also children who have grown up and function out of differing degrees of damage and disfunction. We need to maintain our own quality-controlled thinking about ourselves.

One of the greatest enemies against our integrity is how we see ourselves and think of ourselves. The scripture says, "To love your neighbor as yourself." The question is, then - how can you love others if you don't love yourself first?

In our humanness, we so often can have thoughts of self-loathing, unforgiveness, and bitterness against ourselves. We can take on an attitude of rather than getting something wrong; we start judging ourselves that we are wrong. We step away from our true selves as being sons and daughters of the King and move into an attitude of rebellion and unbelief.

We take on and start to believe the lie from the enemy. This demonic enemy wants to rob us of our actual position where we believe we are not accepted and unworthy. This can lead to resentment, unforgiveness, and even hatred towards ourselves.

HOWYOU.WORK HIRE BEST TALENT.COM

We need good disciplines with our self-talk, to maintain our boundaries of personal protection. We need to hold onto the truth of who we are and our real identity. It is so necessary and important to reconnect with our true selves throughout each day to keep 'short accounts'. Our enemy is always trying to attack us and find a weakness, especially in our own self talk and attitude to self. "Be sober, be vigilant; because your adversary the devil walks about like a roaring lion, seeking whom he may devour" (1 Peter 5:8).

Another good warfare discipline is to know your own God-given identity and how He has designed us. We are incredibly unique and special, and we all have a different purpose and part to play in this life.

A friend of mine, Keith Henry, has spent many years studying the psychology of our gifts, talents and our different forms of intelligence.

We naturally function and perform out of our designed qualities even without realizing it. It is so easy for us to think that performance is our way to be ok.

To excel in any endeavor seems necessary to prove our worthiness to ourselves and all people around us. Performance is the way to be accepted and to be looked upon as being worthy and successful. To be honored and to be looked up to as somebody who is important. The spirit of this world would even cause us to be looked up to as an idol, e.g., movie stars, singers, media personalities, sports stars, etc.

But it is essential to realize there is another side to the coin of performance, where God uses our unique design as a way of celebrating and honoring Him through our individual specialness. It is where we can give back with interest all that God has given.

This is described very well in the scripture relating to the 'parable of the Talents' (Matthew 25:14-30). We have been given gifts and talents, to be used to our full ability and to live life to our full potential to honor the giver of the gift.

The beauty of the principle of giving, especially in your area of gifting and talent, is that you get more in return. Getting this return is not always as you expect it or when you expect it, but it is still a universal truth. This truth will always be honored because God's word says so. It makes it a universally agreed contract that you can trust.

It is still important to remember that we don't give to get. We give out of an attitude of honoring and celebrating what we have been given. This truth comes to us once we realize and agree that we perform out of our specialness and not as a way to gain or receive our specialness.

We have already been born into being unique and special, so relax and enjoy the privilege given to you through God's love.

I used to say to my children, "Just do your best and let God take care of the rest." That is our partnership in action. This is where training and discipline is so important.

Our flesh nature will fight against the truth of being in Godly partnership. The flesh nature wants to isolate and be independent of this partnership. Rather than acknowledging and appreciating our own gifts and talents, we quite often spurn them and want to be like somebody else.

So how can we do our best when we don't have a sense of who we are?

If we cannot understand the nature of our qualities and our design, how can we agree with ourselves and our own specialness when we don't really understand or even know ourselves? This is a huge problem for all of us. How can we set up appropriate boundaries for ourselves in life when we don't even know where we should stand and how we should stand?

We all stand and act differently, because we are different. The world also talks about equality. Equal opportunity is of paramount importance for a fair and equitable society. But nobody is equal. How do you equate or compare apples to oranges? It cannot be done. You can grow them both equally in a good, watered environment where they can grow to their full potential where they are appreciated and enjoyed by all. But they will never be equal, but both are special.

Scripture talks about us being individually in the 'body of Christ', where we all have a different part to play.

1 Corinthians 12:27 says, "Now you are the body of Christ, and members individually." In other words, we all have a special and different part to play in the scheme of life. No two people are the same. We should recognize ourselves and others and celebrate each other's design and purpose.

Romans 12: 4-8 explains this in good detail. "For as we have many members in one body, but all the members do not have the same function, so we, being many, are one body in Christ, and individually members of one another. Having then gifts differing according to the grace that is given to us, let us use them: if prophecy, let us prophesy in proportion to our faith; or ministry, let us use it in our ministering; he who teaches, in teaching; he who exhorts, in exhortation; he who gives, with liberality; he who leads, with diligence; he who shows mercy, with cheerfulness."

My friend, Keith has written a book on the subject and has now completed an app for the family and the community. He named the app 'howyou.work'. His website is called 'Hire best talent.com'.

This program is based on the above scripture from Romans 12. It breaks down our intelligence into nine primary qualities. Then it is broken down to secondary qualities or talents. This program is further unpacked so that individuals can understand more about their strengths and weaknesses. In other words, we learn how to understand and appreciate our own specialness and the specialness of others. So, we can start to appreciate that we don't have to be like somebody else and that other person is not my enemy anymore. We can and should be different from each other in how we think and act.

This more profound understanding of being able to appreciate and agree with our own design helps us move further into our freedom and freeing others to do the same. We can start to work with our differences rather than against them. These are the different intelligent qualities as expressed in Romans 12 and as described in Keith's program.

Achiever, encourager, mentor, carer, giver, practitioner, i.e., (team player) specialist, i.e. (very focussed people), organizers. Ie. (Black-white, right-wrong people) and leaders, i.e., (my way or the highway people). Now these qualities are not cut in stone, we are a mix. But we generally have two qualities that are more dominant. These qualities become a good foundation which can be built upon.

For me, as an example, when I answer the questions in the program, my primary and secondary intelligence or talent always comes out as being an encourager and mentor-teacher.

It is important to realize that understanding your basic qualities does not put you in a tight box. What it does is give you a foundational base to build on. By appreciating and agreeing with your specialness and the specialness of everybody else you encounter will build and grow mutual respect and acceptance.

The boundary component is that we appreciate and accept ourselves and the person next to us. It moves us all into a more profound sense of freedom and empowerment.

Just like the water canal, we are protected and empowered by God's love in us. We can then move mightily in the direction of being life enhancers to ourselves and all people around us. In this, we are all moving forward in the direction set before us. Where we move from strength to strength and glory to glory.

CHAPTER 10

MENTORSHIP

What is it? It means coming alongside somebody because you care. Having the heart to listen and a listening ear, and not judging. Giving gentle supportive advice and being an encourager. Promoting wisdom-based strategies - staying available when needed.

Jesus is our example, and through His Holy Spirit, he is our influence. Jesus met the needs of the people who came to Him, and through meeting their needs, they got to know Him.

In His resurrected body, he said to his disciples, "I am with you always." As Jesus mentors us, we, through his example, may follow in the ministry of mentorship.

In His resurrected body, Jesus came alongside the disciples who were walking to Emmaus. They were walking away from their destiny and purpose. Jesus came to them because He cared for them. Jesus listened to them. He then opened His love and wisdom to them by explaining God's word through the scriptures.

He spoke to their hearts - this caused a change in their hearts and attitudes and caused revelation to their minds. As a result, they were refreshed and fueled up and fired up in their spirit by the Holy Spirit.

In this transformational encounter, they changed direction and moved back into their destiny and their Kingdom purpose in Christ.

This is the blueprint for all of us, the blueprint for mentorship in action - Jesus caring for us and coming alongside us, comes out of His love being expressed. It is His love released in us every day that allows us to come alongside each other because He gives us the capacity to have compassion and care.

In caring with His love, we have His capacity to listen and support our companions as they progress through their life's journey. In moving in this love base, we come alongside and listen to each other. It causes hearts to soften, where defenses start coming down and relationships start to grow.

Choosing to support somebody is a bit like choosing a plant. First you commit to its health and growth by committing to looking after it and watering it. As you do, the plant grows, and the fruit will eventually appear.

God has a way of bringing people around you who will help your growth. This help will come at different times along the journey of life. Yes, character-building goes both ways through mentorship.

My first sense and experiences with mentorship came from my maternal grandfather. As previously said, my grandparents lived with us for seven years and next door to us for seven years. They were always available to help out. They always had a listening ear and would give gentle advice. Mentorship advice helps to grow mutual trust and respect. Yes, it can open up to a lifetime of revelations, life principles and mottos for me and for you.

MENTORSHIP

SHOW ME YOUR FRIENDS AND I'LL SHOW YOU WHAT YOU ARE

I remember two great examples of this with my grandparents. When I was seven, I remember bringing home a boy from my school to play. After a couple of hours, he left.

My grandmother sat me down and looked at me eye to eye, and said, "Mike, show me your friends, and I will show you what you are." Woah! I can still remember her look and what she said. I was only seven but never forgot what she said or what it meant.

Oh, by the way, that boy never came back to my home again. I would often sit with my grandfather. He would often tell me that 'we were Paesanos, which meant we were mates.

WHAT HAPPENS WHEN YOU GET DOWN TO THE LEVEL OF???

One day I was sitting in the gutter outside our home - I was peeved about something that was said or done, and I was sitting down pouting. I used to be able to do a great pout. Haha, my pout came with full-blown cheeks with flared, heavy breathing nostrils. I wish I had a photograph to show you, it was truly a site to behold.

My grandfather sat down next to me. Now you need to know, my grandfather was a Wharfie, a builder, a mechanic, a jack of all trades. He was a beautiful rough diamond. He could do or make anything needed - he was the archetypal Aussie ocker. He even welded my first professional Osteopathic table, which he built 35 years ago, and yes, I am still using it.

Anyway, back to the story at hand. He looked at me squarely in the eye and said, in his vernacular, "Mike, what happens when you get down to the level of shit?"

In my best pouting voice I said, "Whaat?"

He said, "You get it all over you son, stay above it." Woah! Another great motto and principle. Another way of saying this is to use your faith shield and deflect all barbs, falsehoods, and any form of negative rubbish back to God.

God's word says, "Casting all your cares upon him for he cares for you" (1Peter 5:7). I have kept that motto for my life, it has never let me down yet.

Another mentor came into my life when I was twenty-one - it was the time I met Felicity. His name was David, and he mentored many young adults. He was a tennis player as I was. He had driven his daughter and Felicity down to Bega for a tennis tournament. This was where Felicity and I met.

It was God's plan and timing. Through David, I met the girl who would become my wife and the mother of my three children. We are now in our fortieth year of marriage. David also became my Christian mentor, my God father in the Lord. Through him coming along side me I gained an understanding of Christian love. This friend and mentor gave me my first Bible.

David was there for me when in February 1981 my dad, at the age of 49, suddenly died from a heart attack. Having a friend who came alongside me at such a time of bereavement helped lead me in the right direction. I became a born-again Christian in August of that year and married in December.

Through my own experience of being supported and mentored in times of difficulty, you get to understand the power of mentorship. Being led and protected empowers you to trust in life and grow in your own identity and purpose.

Examples of biblical mentors: Moses had Aaron and Hur, Joshua had Moses, Elishah had Elijah, Peter had Jesus, Mark had Peter, Timothy had Paul and on it goes as it should.

MENTORSHIP

NEVER LEAVE YOUR WINGMAN

In the movie 'Top Gun', there was the character 'Maverick'. He was a fighter pilot at the top gun flight school. He was meant to cover his 'wingman'. The motto was, 'You never leave your wingman'.

Unfortunately, Maverick had his own issues and was always trying to prove himself. As a result, he often isolated himself and wasn't a very good team player.

Your wingman always covers you and backs you up, just like a mentor.

It was at a difficult time for 'Maverick'. The commander of the school came alongside Maverick in a mentor capacity. The commander pulled Maverick aside and said, "I would be happy to be your wingman."

Through being mentored and gaining a sense of identity, Maverick understood what it meant to be a true wingman. As a result, his life turned the corner for the better - Maverick went on to mentor many others.

The same goes for each one of us. So, we all need to have a wingman and to be a wingman.

Who are you a wingman for, and who is a wingman for you? Who are you a mentor for and who is your mentor? This position can be for a different person daily. It is a heart attitude to come alongside somebody and back them up and for each of us to be open for someone to do the same for us. In this we help each other grow into our full potential. Through love and care in action, through the heart of mentorship.

CHAPTER 11

The Rule Of The 'Last Run'

In treating many patients over the years especially the ones that play sport, I am always looking at, not only the injury itself but also the cause for the injury.

Cause and Effect. To have an affect there always must be a cause. Our human nature has got a lot to do with the cause and the nature of injuries. These different causes that lead to injury can often be due to us just trying to better ourselves in our performance. It can be our willfulness to gain position or prestige. It can also be due to experiencing the next big adrenal or endorphin high. We are often either trying to prove our worthiness and specialness to ourselves or to impress the people around us.

THE J CURVE PHENOMENA

All of these influences about wanting to give our best and honoring our gifts and talents is normal and ok. The trick is to maintain a degree of balance regarding our 'whys', i.e., our reasons for achievement.

THE RULE OF THE 'LAST RUN'

We need to stay mindful of our protective agendas of fear and pride, so we don't position ourselves too close to the emotional edge of over-protecting ourselves. It is always good to have 'a **margin of error.**', I will say, "Don't forget the 60% rule," to many of my patients.

The meaning of the 60% rule is, decide what you think you can do and then say, 'Great, now what is 60% of that.?" In our need to perform, we will very often try to do too much, eventually to our own detriment. This is why we need a margin of error.

We tend to generally push ourselves and our loved ones beyond limits to get the results that we are looking for. This can be mental and emotional as well as physical over-exertion. We can put so much attention into serving and protecting ourselves through performance that we have nothing left in our proverbial tank to nurture and cover our relationships. It is one of the reasons why so many families suffer due to these emotional and willful imbalances.

A glaring example of not adhering to the 60% rule was one Christmas eve when I decided for us as a family to rush down and drive to Melbourne to visit my sister and her family, before they were rushing off the next day to go to Tasmania.

I got home late from work and finished packing the car by midnight. I had two hours sleep, then bundled Felicity and my three young children into the car and took off to Melbourne.

By the time we got to Albury, I was exhausted. I decided to stop for lunch, believing that having something to eat would give me the energy to keep driving. It's amazing how reckless, willful agendas can cause you to move into willful, dangerous denial and you don't even recognize it.

After I got my sugar hit we took off straight away onto the Victorian freeway.

My eyes started to close involuntarily.

Suddenly a flight attendant on the bus said,

"do you want to stay on the bus or get off"? Whaaat!

At that point my wise, mindful wife dug me in the ribs and said " your eyes were closed"!

I had fallen asleep at the wheel. In a blink I could of wiped out my whole family. Another road statistic.

Thank God for His grace and mercy and Felicity's mindful discernment.

Not adhering to the 'rule of the last run' and the 60% rule in this case could of been deadly.

From an athletic point of view, many will push themselves without realizing they are moving into the 'red zone of fatigue'. In this zone people are setting themselves up for injury. It causes many never to see their full potential as they create the 'J curve' phenomena, pushing themselves too far and then crashing.

Unfortunately, all injuries generally leave a mark, emotionally as well as physically. It will often lead people to need clinical help to overcome their limitations formed by the nature of inflammation and the formation of scar tissue. It causes tissue hardening and inflexibility, which can lead to further chronic damage. These injuries don't have to be just physical, but also mental, emotional and relational.

I had one patient who was a gifted athlete. He would always want to improve and perfect his skills. However, in this refinement towards perfection, there is a downside. By striving for higher performance and greater results, we can put our body in harm's way. Our margin of error gets finer and finer and with this comes the increased potential of injury.

This patient over the years had many injuries. I said to him once, "You know, adrenaline will take you so far, and then it will kill you."

I have had patients that I am so sad to say, who have died from pushing the envelope of performance too far.

Sometimes the 'highs' of life can become our goal. But unfortunately, sometimes that desire goes too far, and it becomes an idol. The highs can become our drug, and as the effect of drugs, we are always looking for the next high, which is never enough and will never satisfy.

As the line of life gets more refined, so does the point of balance, between ok and not, ok. Also, between good and bad, right and wrong, in danger or out of danger, in harmony not in harmony, and on we go.

THE RULE OF THE LAST RUN

Over the years, I used to treat a lot of patients who were preparing to go to the ski fields. I used to say to them, "Whatever you do, lookout and be careful on your last run."

My own experience with skiing would soon cause me to change my wording to my patients.

I was skiing with friends. It was our third day on the ski fields, and I was starting to feel confident. The icicles on the trees, the sun radiating on my face, and the cold breeze on my cheeks, 'perrfect'. We were at the top of the mountain, and it was the last run before lunch. As I took off down the slope, I could feel my adrenaline pumping in. and I started to go faster and faster.

Halfway down the mountain, I hit the moguls. Again, I stayed low in my squat position and maintained the pace. I remember feeling my 'quads' begin to burn from a lactic acid build up. But that didn't deter me or slow me down - achieving my downhill run goal was at stake.

Suddenly I was at the finish line. I had beaten the mountain, my friends, and even the moguls. I was king of the mountain, yay! I slowed down to go in for my well-deserved lunch. But then I saw a little ski jump formed over a couple of little rocks, out of the corner of my right eye. This ski jump was screaming at me, "Have a go!" So, I veered over to the jump. In the changing of my direction, I had slowed down. But I had committed to finishing my thrill on a high note. So, I went into a slight squat position and hit the jump.

Rather than an exhilarating uplift, my body was starting to collapse. I could feel both my legs beginning to give way. Both my knees started to twist in opposite directions. My ability to control the situation had sadly and painfully gone. Because I had slowed down, my bindings didn't release. Of course, the ensuing force kept on building up to an excruciating pain wracking, cracking crescendo on both my knee joints.

I started to cry out in agony as I heard a large cracking sound in both knees, as my cruciate ligaments tore away. There I was, an agonizing, humbled heap in the snow, in considerable pain, lying under the chair lifts with the uncaring world looking on. Well, that's not entirely true - as a good friend Kerry, was looking out for me and saw my calamitous fall from grace and helped me limp off the ski field. A more broken and humbled man! This life will humble us, one way or the other. 1 Peter 5:6 says, "Therefore humble yourselves under the mighty hand of God, that He may exalt you in due time."

The cause for this painful calamity relates to adrenaline. You are so high on adrenaline you don't recognize your body's warning signals that you are totally exhausted.

Haha, just like my surfing career and horse-riding career, I realized I just finished my skiing career. Oh, how pride and too much adrenaline cometh before a fall.

After my six months of recovery, the old statement that I used to say to my patients changed dramatically. My new word to patients was, "What happens when you get to your last run?"

"YOU DON'T DO IT!"

You are already shot from exhaustion, as you use your 'fatigue speech' and say, last run or last anything. Believe me and go straight into the lodge or onto the beach etc. Put your feet up, say well done and have a well-deserved drink.

THE RULE OF THE 'LAST RUN'

As I look back at all my injuries through many different sporting activities, I realized that they all happened in my early forties. I realized I must have been going through the emotional trauma of a mid-life crisis.

I remember that on top of that, around the same time frame, I bought a Mazda MX5 convertible, to my wife's dismay. In my defense, I might add, I had my 'last run' with my MX5, and I only kept my fun car for three months. to satisfy my midlife emotional damage, which is another story.

"For he who has an ear to hear."

CHAPTER 12

There Is Always A Price To Be Paid

I used to say to my children is that "Whatever you do in this life, there's a price to be paid, sometimes sooner, sometimes later, but there is always a price."

There is a saying, 'the apple doesn't fall far from the tree.'

I used to call my son Jeremy the 'wild stallion' he would leap and then look. When he was a toddler, I would say to him, "Jez, you've only got one body." As he got older, I told him, "Jez think before you do things." As he got older again my words were, "Jez wisdom before excitement." Later I said, "Mate, you've got to improve your margin of error."

Jez has always had a beautiful big heart. He has always given his best even to his own physical detriment.

I remember saying at his twenty first birthday.

That Jeremy reminded me of a hero, but heros get killed.

I remember Jez playing Rugby Union, running up the wing, side stepping and dummying three players and scoring a try. This feat was achieved whilst trying to protect a dislocated shoulder. This shoulder condition was achieved due to dirt bike riding while attempting to bypass a big tree.

"As I said before, the 'apple doesn't fall far from the tree'.

Jeremy had a few of my generational traits. As a teenager the need to perform and to be accepted through good works was an ongoing position which led him to exhaustion. This caused Jez to suffer anxiety issues and panic attacks.

Jeremy through perseverance and faith based persistence learned how to humble himself before God. Through amazing grace Jez moved into his healing and freedom and learned how to go from strength to strength.

Through his experiences Jeremy wrote a book titled "180 degree Anxiety". He has tamed down on his sporting injuries and now plays a great game of golf. (James 4:10) "Humble yourself in the sight of the Lord and He will lift you up".

My beautiful youngest son is now thirty-four years old. He has had three knee reconstructions, and his left shoulder is not much behind.

But my little hero has survived it all and is now flourishing as a man of God. He is an excellent teacher.

Jeremy comes along side his students showing the father heart of God through expressing an open heart of communication and mutual respect. He is ministering and teaching Christian studies and doing chaplaincy. Through his big heart and life experiences, he is helping many more young men to grow and find their true selves and leading them in their journey of faith to achieve their full potential in this world.

Interestingly, there is a scripture that speaks of learning and growing through our experiences.

Through paying the price we can grow strong and strengthen others as well.

It says in (2 Corinthians 1:3-4), "Blessed be the God and Father of our Lord Jesus Christ, the Father of mercies and God of all comfort, who comforts us in all our tribulation, that we may be able to comfort those who are in any trouble, with the comfort with which we ourselves are comforted by God."

This scripture expresses the reality that as we grow and learn to pay the price through the trials and errors of our life we can sympathize and support others who are going through similar experiences in their journey.

Riding along this lifes journey with Jeremy is his beautiful wife, Rachel.

Hand in hand they are building and growing each other. Rache's sensitivity and wisdom coupled with Jez's strength, encouragement and go for it attitude, makes them a couple that together will impart and minister these qualities to all.

Jeremy is no longer the wild stallion. He has changed through much growth through trial and error, learning and growing through God's Grace, coupled with his heart to never give up, to do the hard yards, and pay the price of faith, hope and love. He is now the amazing war horse. Good on you Jez.

'KGFI' (KEEP GOING FOR IT)

Life and change go together. Scripture says that in life, through the good choices we make, we can grow and change from 'strength to strength and glory to glory'.

To cause this change we need to make micro decisions on a moment-by-moment basis.

The funny thing is that in our human nature we generally don't like change.

Change often makes us feel uncomfortable. Change moves us from a known experiential point of view into the 'dreaded' unknown. This is especially difficult for the thoughtful 'organizer' – melancholics amongst us.

THERE IS ALWAYS A PRICE TO BE PAID

The fear of the 'what if's' can plague our minds - it can make us feel insecure and vulnerable. The reason for this is we can't get a handle on the situation, and we, therefore, think that we are not in control.

Parents can often function out of fear and go down the 'what if' scenario for their children, which is very understandable. But trying to protect your kids from all of life's situations and scenarios is unrealistic, unsustainable and, as I experienced, very exhausting.

For our kids' sake, let's not stifle them out of our position of fear.

Let's trust God for our children. They are His before they are ours. We should partner with God and practice making decisions for them based on God's lead. So, as we partner with God for our kids, let's trust in faith and hope rather than fear.

IF GOD, HAS IT SORTED, YOU DON'T HAVE TO SORT IT.

I was thinking of my three children and how different they all are in their design, as we all are. They all had the same upbringing but all so different. 'Made on purpose for a purpose'.

It is important that we believe in the overriding plan and purpose for each of us so that we trust, as we move and work with the current of life.

Then, we won't act out of fear and try to force ourselves or our loved ones to swim against the current of life.

If we don't get God's lead, we will go in the wrong fruitless directions and just get exhausted. God's way empowers us with grace which allows us to get through the hard yards without getting tired, frustrated, and more fearful.

Remember, "His perfect Love casts out fear" (1 John 4:18).

My eldest son Phil is naturally reserved and analytical and has a great dry wit. He is a lot of fun.

As a young boy, he would ponder and think things out. When he was confident with his thoughts, he would then verbalize them.

I remember when he was in primary school, he didn't want to go in the school swimming carnival for two years

Knowing Phil's mind, we knew it was not suitable to coerce or force him when his mind was set.

We just trusted in the process of life that it would sort out.

This was the case with Phil. The next year come around. Phil said, "I'm racing today."

Well, what a powerhouse. He blitzed every race.

With his analytical mind, he simply needed time to work out what he needed to do and how to do it. Then, with a bit of practice, he moved into his confidence and became a state swimmer.

It is good to know that if you trust and believe that God has it sorted, then you don't have to sort it.

It certainly takes the pressure and stress out of the differing circumstances of life.

Another time Phil was about twelve years of age. He was going through a phase where he didn't like us going out. He would carry on a treat. Of course, we realized that it was the fear of the unknown and maybe the concern of feeling responsible but not knowing what to do. Ha, such is the life of an organizer - melancholic.

Ps; For more info on our different talents and intelligences, go to the app, 'howyou.work' and speak to my friend, Keith Henry.

After a few weeks of Phil distressing and having a few other fear episodes, I decided we had to deal with this spirit of fear. "For God has not given us a spirit of fear, but of power and of love and of a sound mind "(2 Timothy 1:7).

It is important to understand, many emotional episodes can come from a spiritual, or more to the point, a demonic source. These demonic attacks can come upon us from open doors that we activate through taking on negative attitudes and damaging thinking.

THERE IS ALWAYS A PRICE TO BE PAID

A lot of these stressors come on from unrequited griefs and traumas from the past. Through these open portals that we create, through attitudes of fear, we give demonic spirits opportunity, authority, and free reign to come in and attack us and our loved ones.

MY OWN FEAR ENCOUNTER

When Jeremy, our youngest, was five, I was putting him to bed.

Jeremy said to me, "Dad I'm scared of dying." I said we should pray about that.

I moved into a spiritual warfare prayer for Jez to break that generational curse off him. At the same time, I felt led to pray for myself as well.

I then went to bed.

Suddenly an attack came on. I was in another spiritual dream. I could feel a sense of pressure on me physically. It was like Satan himself was trying to strangle me. I could feel physical pressure on my neck while still in this visionary dream state.

I was able to squeak out the statement of authority, "In the name of Jesus."

Suddenly the visionary scene in the dream had changed. I could feel a physical vibration of healing running through my body. There was this incredible sense of peace over me, like a protective force field.

As I was bathing in this new sensation, I noticed that I was sitting on a park bench under what looked like a covering of large sprawling willow trees. I also noticed that opposite me were two other park benches. I also noticed there was a person sitting on each bench.

As I was still feeling this warm healing sensation like a vibration on my physical body, while still in my dream state, I thought to myself, "Who are they?"

Straight away the person opposite me on the left bench said, "My name is Gabriel."

In my dream I thought, "That's cool."

Straight away my next thought was, "I wonder who the other guy is?"

He responded straight away and said, "My name is Jasper." I thought again that was cool.

By this stage I had woken up. I could still feel this healing vibration happening in my body.

It was 3:00 am. I got out of bed and was praying and giving thanks for this amazing spiritual experience and breakthrough.

Then I stopped and thought to myself, "Who is Jasper?"

I thought to myself, "Well God if this is real, there must be something in the Bible to back this one up."

So, there I was in the dark with the old-style Strong's Concordance, looking for the word Jasper.

As I looked down the list, suddenly, there was 'Jasper'. Jasper is the foundational stone of Heaven.

So, I believe Jasper is a foundational angel in the heavenly realm and is also one of my protecting angels.

So, thank you for your faithful backup Gabriel and Jasper. It is most welcomed and appreciated.

GET GOD'S DOWNLOAD

So as far as dealing with your own spiritual warfare attacks. Get God's download.

Some of these entities, these powers, and principalities can enter our domain from generational curses.

Ask God to give you His Spiritual discernment and knowledge. Get God's warfare strategy on how to bind them and cast them off you and your household. They must be cut off, smashed, and kicked out of your life. Get them off you and your loved ones and move into your

God-given ordained authority and move you and your family into your future and hope.

PRAYER MODEL- paraphrased from 'Wellspring Ministries'.

"Heavenly Father in Jesus Name, forgive me for taking on a spirit of------- thankyou that I am forgiven.

Heavenly Father I claim back my authority over all demonic spirits that have attacked me because I am forgiven. I bind them and cast them out in Jesus Name.

Heavenly Father heal my heart from all trauma, fill me with your amazing grace and lead me in your truth and understanding, Amen."

Back to Phil. I received God's download and strategy. I knew I needed to help Phil act and experience the reality of his authority in Christ Jesus. It was time that he took back his authority.

I took him by the arm and marched him into the bathroom, shut the door, and said to him, "Now I want you to yell out as loud as you can. 'PISS OFF SATAN.' Go on, say it, say it louder, 'PISS OFF SATAN,' say it louder, 'PISS OFF SATAN.'

Six years later, when Phil did his first sermon at Bible College, guess what his first sermon was on? Haha, you guessed it.

The only way to re-establish our rightful authority and close the doors on these evil infiltrators is through paying the price, through repentance and forgiveness. Repent to God for what we have allowed in and seek forgiveness for our thoughts or actions and also forgiving others for theirs.

Through prayer and faith Phil took authority over the enemy. In Phil's case it was the spirit of fear.

He also conquered agoraphobia. Being in a room full of people was a major struggle, or even worse - if he had to get into a lift, that was the worst. The demon of claustrophobia would take over.

The price to be paid was believing and not doubting that he could beat this condition. This moved Phil into hope.

"Faith is the substance of things **hoped** for, the evidence of things not seen" (Hebrews 11:1).

Believing for breakthrough and not doubting moves us all into the realm of faith which can move any type of mountain, Including agoraphobia and claustrophobia (Matthew 21:21-22).

From Phil's new position of authority in Christ, he grew strong and took up many new challenges.

He started to learn bass guitar. This was under the training and mentorship of our youth Pastor, Richie. Out of this relationship, Phil grew more in confidence and more in character.

The love of Christ through building relationships, waters the plant, the roots go deeper into the soil of Godly character.

When Felicity and I decided to go to a different church, Phil at the age of seventeen stayed on to support his youth pastor. Good on you Phil, character is formed out of the refining process of life.

Phil grew in confidence, became vice captain of the school and headed up youth ministry.

This led him on to do full time training as a youth minister then pastor.

It's amazing that as we step out in faith other parts of life seem to fit together. "As we step, God moves".

In Phil's case while doing ministry training, he met his beautiful wife to be, Lucy, she was at the time doing creative ministry.

Lucy has a great strength about her and a very caring heart. She is a wonderful singer and song writer.

Their great affinity to support and comfort each other grew a strong bond that they now use mightily together to grow others.

This reminds me of that same scripture that was for Jeremy. Maybe it is for all of us!

THERE IS ALWAYS A PRICE TO BE PAID

(2 Corinthians 1:3-4) says, blessed be the God and Father of our Lord Jesus Christ, the Father of mercies and God of all comfort, who comforts us in all our tribulation, that we may be able to comfort those who are in any trouble, with the comfort with which we ourselves are comforted by God.

As we are strengthened through trusting God as we go through our own trials, we are then equipped and able to support others through their similar trials.

It is good to remember that sometimes in our own journey, it is not always about us.

We grow stronger, building our faith muscle through our trials, then we are more equipped to identify with others. We can then help them along the way to also grow their faith muscle and breakthrough themselves.

In Phil's case, he now rides the heavily crowded tubes of London. He pastors a church in London with his wife Lucy. They pass on the amazing grace gained through believing and trusting in each other and in God through paying the price.

'Good one Phil, (KGFI) 'Keep going for it'.

Every day we can move into our God given authority, given to us through Jesus Christ.

Matt 28:18-20 proclaims, "And Jesus came and spoke to them, saying, 'All authority has been given to Me in heaven and on earth. Go therefore and make disciples of all the nations, baptizing them in the name of the Father and of the Son and of the Holy Spirit, teaching them to observe all things that I have commanded you; and lo, I am with you always, even to the end of the age.' Amen."

We can then tell Satan 'Where to go' in no uncertain terms through our authority in and only in Christ.

We are all very differently designed, and with this comes diverse ways of thinking and acting.

Understanding and appreciating and respecting our differences can take us a long way in growing and strengthening ourselves and all our relationships.

HOLD ON TO THE HUGS OF LIFE

An important scripture to remember is in Jeremiah 29:11, where God says, "For I know the thoughts and plans I think toward you, says the Lord, thoughts of peace and not of evil, to give you a future and a hope."

Let this knowledge build you up in faith and hope and move you away from the fear of the 'what ifs' and anxiety.

In life, we can cause change or change can come upon us. In either case we need to look at options, weigh up the 'pros and cons', become strategic, pay the price, make decisions, step out in faith and act on those decisions.

Our daughter Angie was our firstborn.

I remember her as a six-month-old. Felicity had a few days away with her mum and sister.

I picked them up at the airport, which very busy at the time.

Felicity was holding Ange. I could see that Ange even then was looking very intently at all the crowd, being discerning, analyzing and asking the 'why' questions. The 'why' question has always been a strong part of Angie's design.

Suddenly she recognized me through all the crowd. A big smile came on her face, and she put her arms out for a big hug. It was Ange, wanting to give me a big hug. It was a hug that lasts a lifetime - a great memory. Angie's hugs are not just physical - they are proverbial hugs from the heart, which ministers to everyone who meets her.

Ange is still the same today. She has a great smile and gives life a big hug with all she has got. Life is certainly better for all the people who have received and experienced Angie's life enhancing hugs.

DO YOUR BEST LET GOD TAKE CARE OF THE REST

Ange is very multi-talented and gifted. She studied music, then she studied interior design, and then she studied journalism. She has a mind like a 'steel trap'.

As an athlete, she could beat the boys at push-ups and sit ups.

She was asked to swim butterfly in a school carnival once, as nobody else wanted to give it a go. Of course, the bait that was dangled to Angie was getting more points for the school.

She had never swum butterfly before but was always willing to try. Paying the price comes in all shapes and sizes.

She won the race and swam butterfly perfectly - who does that? She then swam butterfly in the state.

I remember when Angie's youth pastors, Glenn and Clare, came to us at church. They said, "You have to come down to the classroom and listen to Angie sing." We did. Tears came to our eyes. It was as if we were listening to an angel, which made sense.

Angie became a jazz singer. She always had a desire to produce a jazz album.

When she felt the time was right, in a three-month period, she rallied musicians around her and produced her own jazz album - what an achievement. It was a beautiful album called,

'Some Kind of Daydream'.

Why am I telling you all this?

Life takes many turns. Are we willing to pay the price, to step out in faith and try, and go through the pain and sacrifice that is always a part of paying the price?

Angie eventually became a very good and very successful TV producer.

This life journey has many twists and turns, up and downs, what I call the hills and valleys of the journey of life. But the most important thing to know is when you say to Jesus, "I want you to walk with me." That is exactly what He will do.

You don't have to make this journey on your own. Jesus says in Matthew 28, "I am with you always." When you take in that reality, you can have His peace no matter what the circumstances may be.

His grace empowers you to pay the price.

This journey of life also has 'T' intersections. A 'T' intersection is a point in time where you realize that "I can't go in the same direction anymore." You ask the question, "Will I go right, or will I go left?"

The price is you must choose. So, that becomes your step of faith, where you are again moving forward.

In Angie's case, her 'T' intersection was, that after twelve years of doing long twelve hour shifts under much pressure as a TV producer, her physical body came to a screeching halt. The ongoing stress had pushed her adrenal system into so much ongoing overload and exhaustion that her body went into physiological shut down, known as 'adrenal fatigue'.

Angie's body and lifestyle had to be recalibrated.

It was a daily struggle to lift her head, let alone get out of bed.

As a dad and mum, we were on call every day for around twelve months to be available for whatever it took. It is the price you pay as a parent. The 'journey of the hills and valleys' with all your children is an ongoing labor of love. Thank goodness for God's endless empowering grace.

God's amazing grace is also found in the loved ones that partner us through life. In Angie's case it is her beautiful husband, Daniel.

Daniel's gentle loving spirit came to the fore time and time again. He was Ange's true day by day lifeguard, nurse, amazing cook, counsellor, taxi driver and confidant.

God truly empoved Dan every day through His sacrificial love. Strengthening Ange in every way including their marriage. To have a loving partner like Dan to back you up in the trenches of life is a true blessing and a great example of how we are to position ourselves for marriage and life generally.

Good job Dan KGFI.

Angie was 35 years old at the time. You never stop being a parent. After about six months of recovery, Ange started to do short walks down the street and back.

On many occasions, Angie would call us, saying, "I've walked down the street, but I can't get back."

Like debits and credits on a graph sheet, each decision we make will cause us to keep moving through the highs and lows, the journey of the hills and valleys of life.

The price we need to pay may be the price of discipline, of wisdom, of patience, of being strategic, of listening, of self-control. Listening is a good one, as we have two ears and one mouth, we should therefore listen twice as much as we speak.

Paying the price early helps us to move forward with strong mindsets, emotional stability, and strong spiritual foundations for building a life of favor and integrity. Paying the price later usually means fixing crumbled foundations, due to them being built on unstable thought processing.

A good, useful principle in paying the price early is the price of submitting to God's will. Remember that He is still your business partner. The Lord created you, knows you, loves you, and always has your best interest at heart.

The other price in this process, is choosing to trust.

If you struggle trusting, then pay the price, which is - ask to receive more love so you can trust.

The price of thinking and asking before you do things has many merits.

So, in this life journey of so many choices, pay the price and talk to God.

The price will certainly be worth it.

With Angie's recovery, that is exactly what she had to do. Changes needed to be made.

The price to be paid was medical support and psychological support.

Through Angie's health journey, she came to another 'T' intersection.

In her learning so much about how to regain her own health, she has now decided to embark on a new journey to help others find their health. At the age of 37, Angie has now left the TV producing industry and has gone back to Uni to study medical science and become a health professional, to pass on what she has learned and help others.

Again, that scripture comes true once again. 2 Corinthians 1:3-4 says, "Blessed be the God and Father of our Lord Jesus Christ, the Father of mercies and God of all comfort, who comforts us in all our tribulation, that we may be able to comfort those who are in any trouble, with the comfort with which we ourselves are comforted by God.

'Go Pange, your another 'life enhancer', KGFI, Love Dad."

CHAPTER 13

You're Not A Castle, You're A Temple

Castles were built primarily for security, protection, pride and power. The price for building these amazing edifices was the ongoing focused energy, time, money and labor required to complete and then to maintain such a protective edifice.

The reason for building these castles was that the enemy would see these protective barriers and the powers behind them. They would be so intimidated by this display of power, will and might that they would stay away. These castles would have to be constantly maintained at great cost for peace to be achieved.

But as life would have it and history shows, peace was never maintained very long as enemies were always surrounding you and always looking for ways to attack you and bring you down. So, in time most castles become ruins, as life has its way of knocking down our man-made edifices.

It is so often the same in our own lives. We can put all our energies into building great walls of protection against all forms of possible invasion into the inner sanctum of our hearts. In doing this, we try to protect our heartfelt position at all costs.

Our castle is a castle of fear, bitterness, resentment, rejection, of loss, and insecurity. We try to hold onto our sense of power, control, pride, greed, ego, and on we go.

We get caught up in protecting ourselves financially through how much money I can earn. Prestige - how big a house I can have. Security - how many homes can I buy? Power - how many people can I control and influence?

Don't get me wrong; they are all very good and valid achievements. Scripture tells us in 1 Timothy 6:10, "The love of money is a root to all kinds of evil." So, the issue is not wealth or possessions in themselves, but our attitude toward them, will make or break us.

ARE YOU COMFORTABLE IN YOUR OWN SKIN?

So, my thought to you is, right now, in this moment and in the space, you are in, are you comfortable in your skin? Or how much room do you need between four walls to be comfortable?

So, our comfort should not be based on the size or the quality of our surroundings or what you are wearing or the type of car you're driving or how much money you have in the bank. Our comfort should be based on the degree of peace that we have in our hearts from one moment to the next.

Scripture tells us in 1 Corinthians 6:19-20: 19. "Or do you not know that your body is the temple of the Holy Spirit who is in you, whom you have from God, and you are not your own? 20. For you were bought at a price; therefore, glorify God in your body and in your spirit, which are God's." Our true home is our heart position in God and His position in us.

Matthew 6:19-21 says, "Do not lay up for yourselves treasures on earth, where moth and rust destroy and where thieves break in and steal; but lay up for yourselves treasures in heaven, where neither moth nor rust destroys and where thieves do not break in and steal. For where your treasure is, there your heart will be also."

Where is your treasure? Is it eternally lasting or very fleeting? This life of ours goes in a blink. Is it time to readjust your priorities?

We who have faith in Jesus, we have become His earthly temple, we carry Christ in us. Colossians 1:27 - "Christ in you the hope of Glory."

1Corinthians 6:19-20, "Or do you not know that your body is the temple of the Holy Spirit who is in you, whom you have from God, and you are not your own? For you were bought at a price; therefore, glorify God in your body and in your spirit, which are God's.

As disciples of Jesus, we are the temple for His Holy Spirit. We house the Holy Spirit of God in us. We dwell, and abide in Him, and He dwells in us. Through our relationship with God through Jesus Christ as our Savior, we carry the peace that transcends all understanding that guards our hearts and minds. (Philippian's 4:7). This peace is the manifestation of our true freedom that removes all the constraints of the world. These constraints would try to control us and pressurize us to continue to build monolithic emotional castles of distress, denial, exhaustion, and despair.

Even now, at this moment, ask Jesus into your heart to be your Lord and Savior. Ask right now to receive Jesus Christ into your heart afresh. Receive His Holy Spirit into your heart. Let go and repent of all the castles of control, rejection, fear, pride bitterness and self-hatred you have built over the years to protect yourself. Give them all over to God and let them go now and be a temple for God's Holy Spirit. Give thanks for receiving His peace into your heart and celebrate with Him as you move into your freedom. Amen.

CHAPTER 14

The Grief Industry

Individuals, villages, tribes, nations, the human race! Scripture talks about the flesh lusting against the spirit. Another terminology for this is enmity or waring. "Beloved, I beg you as sojourners and pilgrims, abstain from fleshly lusts which war against the soul" (1 Peter 2:11).

Another flesh terminology is to be carnal. Romans 8:5-8 says, "For those who live according to the flesh set their minds on the things of the flesh, but those who live according to the Spirit, the things of the Spirit. For to be carnally minded is death, but to be spiritually minded is life and peace. Because the carnal mind is enmity against God; for it is not subject to the law of God, nor indeed can be. So then, those who are in the flesh cannot please God."

THE GOOD NEWS IS...

But God looks to the heart. 1 Samuel 16:7 - "But the LORD said to Samuel, 'Do not look at his appearance or at his physical stature, because I have refused him. For the LORD does not see as man sees; for man looks at the outward appearance, but the LORD looks at the heart.'"

WE ARE NOT HUMAN DOINGS; WE ARE HUMAN BEINGS THAT DO.

Our doings should be a natural outcome out of our being in Christ. In the book of James 1:22, It speaks of being a doer of the word. This produces the good fruit, which grows out of our being.

As God is a God of relationship, he looks to each one of our hearts with a heart of love. We are designed to do the same thing - tap into His wellspring of love and then express that love and seed it wherever we go. It produces good fruit in others wherever we go.

So why is it so difficult to look from the love base of our hearts and the hearts of those around us? Why is it so difficult to produce good fruit?

In our damage, our flesh nature goes into protection mode. We start to guard ourselves against dealing with the pains of life. We go into the protective posture of denial. We look for fault in others to deflect from our own damage, so we can feel to be ok with ourselves. We start to medicate ourselves from a place of feelings rather than faith. We get so caught up in protecting ourselves from our own pain that we can't recognize the pain in others or ourselves.

It's called '**THE DROWNING MAN SYNDROME**'

We stay in a state of denial where we don't even recognize that we are drowning. In the swirling waves of our dysfunctions and pain we compensate by finding fault in others and pushing them down in the dark waters of our own damage. In doing this, we try to raise ourselves higher through egocentric pride, manipulative control, fault finding and putting others down all in order to keep ourselves afloat. This is called the 'Aussie knocker' syndrome.

In such a state, we get ourselves exhausted. Eventually, we all drown. In performance-based living we try to get our ok-ness through doing. The more you do the more you've got to do because the goal mouth of worldly values keeps changing. We always have to achieve more to be accepted. Then the 'tall poppy syndrome' comes into play to knock you down again. We keep being asked to jump into more hoops. It all becomes very exhausting.

OUR HEART IS THE COMPASS OF THE SOUL

Our heart is the compass of our soul. Therefore, the heart can be attracted and led by our spirit towards God. Our heart compass can also be attracted to the flesh nature, which is influenced by the spirit of this world, Satan, where he leads us towards further damage and destruction.

In this self-centering, we become the central target. Every negative thought comes back at us like a hurtling missile. Whether it is self-speaking or speaking about others, our heart is the target that the enemy wants to destroy.

To cope with the sense of rejection and abandonment due to the ongoing bombardment against our hearts, we start to play the 'blame game'. "It is your fault that I am in this state or situation." We then play the 'you owe me' game. The eternal cycle of shame, grief, rejection, anger, unforgiveness, and bitterness goes on and on.

Each one of these flesh symptoms blocks love. Our 'heart compass' hardens through the inflammatory nature of emotional distress. It makes the heart compass turn more to the flesh nature and is then more influenced by the demonic forces that cling onto flesh attitudes.

In this cycle, we become more defensive to protect our damaged hearts. We struggle more and more to receive love and to give love. In this state, on a physical level, negative emotions and stressors will damage our physiological capacities through increased inflammatory responses to the nervous system and the immune system.

Even our physical hearts harden as all these influences affect our immune system. This inflammation can lead to hardening of our arteries. As a result, our physical bodies deteriorate in like manner.

As we look to Jesus and ask for help, he will lift us out of the swirling waters of distress and despair. His Grace then empowers us to repent before God and to forgive ourselves and others. Galatians 5:16 – "I say then: Walk in the Spirit, and you shall not fulfill the lust of the flesh."

The past is in the past. The future is in the future. This moment is a gift, that's why it's called the 'present'. Forgiveness then moves us out of living in the griefs of the past. This allows us to be fully present in the present moment where we can progress unencumbered into moving forward through hope to a blessed future.

CHAPTER 15

Are Your Oil Lamps Full?

Have you ever been driving on a lonely road in the middle of the night, and suddenly, your car lights just go out? Woah! That happened to me once, very scary. High beam on, a straight road in front of me and 'wham'! The electrics go out. All sense of comfort and security is gone.

So is an empty oil lamp in the journey of life. Your whole sense of clarity, direction, ok-ness, endurance and hope, gone.

Before electricity, oil lamps were the only means to see in the dark. Without the ability to ignite fire from the oil, there was no way of moving forwards in the darkness of night. Without the oil, it was like you were walking blind, fearing what could be behind you and what was ahead of you or what could be around the corner.

The insecurity of the darkness of despair, helplessness, and hopelessness is always a concern. Not being able to rely on anybody - on your own and desperate for a light to direct you out of your dire predicament of being stuck. All bearings of being safe are gone. You are not even able to feel your way out and being in the dark - blind terror!

So, there would be no moving forwards. You stay stagnant in fear, anxiety, frustration, and despair. You are turned off to the light through the grief of the past. So, it is in the darkness of this day and age. The grief of the past poisoning your present and blocking you from a functional future.

The 'woke' and 'cancel culture', and the humanists of this world, empowered by the spirit of the Antichrist would like to keep everybody in the dark. Promoting a godless grief ridden culture, where control is the name of the game.

This present darkness has taken over the media. This world thrives off media and entertainment, where gossip and character assassinations are part of the game. They blame everything on the errors of the past, blocking forward movement and stifling our future through lowest case denominator thinking.

Oil is the fuel which produces the needed light for spiritual survival. This oil speaks of the Holy Spirit, who is the Spirit of God. God's Spirit that has been given as a gift to all believers who have received Jesus Christ as their Lord and Savior.

The Holy Spirit is the reservoir of refreshing, the fuel that empowers us into love, joy, peace, patience, grace, and mercy. The Holy Spirit is the seal of our security and confidence. He is our life resource that allows us to see in the dark.

Through belief and obedience in God's word, there is ignition. His light is turned on in you, then darkness disappears. He gives us empowering grace for all situations. He is the fuel that fires us up to do great things.For us to carry on strong in Him no matter where we are and what is happening on the road of this life journey.

If you are not a believer in Jesus Christ as Lord and Savior, you don't have the Holy Spirit. You can only use your own limited resources. In this you receive your empowerment from the spirit of this world and all the lusts thereof. The light of this world will eventually turn off, and then what?

The resource of this world is like a car shaking and spluttering on the last few dregs of dirty fuel. The battery of worldly excitement is going dead. The electrics of living without true empowerment are short circuiting.

Matthew 25:1-5, "Then the kingdom of heaven shall be likened to ten virgins who took their lamps and went out to meet the bridegroom. Now five of them were wise, and five were foolish. Those who were foolish took their lamps and took no oil with them, But the wise took oil in their vessels with their lamps. But while the bridegroom was delayed, they all slumbered and **slept**," ie (to be overcome or oppressed, to yield to sloth and sin, to be indifferent to one's salvation). 'Sleep' is also a euphemism for being dead.

The virgins heard a cry at midnight that the bridegroom was coming, and they went to trim their lamps, but the foolish virgin's lamps were going **out** i.e, (to quench, to suppress, stifle of divine influence).

Today, the times are getting darker. It is midnight, and the cry is going out, 'Prepare'. Only the light of Christ can expel the darkness of a world that is imploding on itself. We need to tap into the unlimited reserves of the oil of God's Holy Spirit every day.

We are then able to move in His authority, power, grace, and mercy. This gives us the capacity to cope and rise above all the traumas and attacks that come our way in a world that is on the path of self-destruction.

Putting our heads in the sand or staying in denial won't change the direction of the downward spiral of this world. The good news is, that all you have to do is ask God to cleanse your heart. Ask Him to take the hardness out and give you a 'heart of flesh'.

Forgiveness and repentance are how you trim the wick of faith. It removes and cleans all the soot of this world off your damaged heart. Then your wick of faith will draw up the oil of life and through obedience to

God's word you can relight your spirit and power up your soul and pass it on to others.

Now that's something to cheer about and get excited about. This is where you will seek after God, and His Holy Spirit will come to the door of your heart. He will knock on this door. The door of seeking, the door of wanting to understand, the door of communion and relationship. The door of faith and life. Open the door of your heart to God, even now. Ask Him into your heart and fill it afresh with His love.

Jesus says, "Behold, I stand at the door and knock. If anyone hears My voice and opens the door, I will come into him and dine with him, and he with Me" (Revelation 3:20).

It's time to hear the midnight call. Through the grace of the Holy Spirit, we can enter into the Kingdom of His love. Let him fill you with the oil of His love. As you invite Him into your heart, the light of His love will be instantly turned on, and all darkness will disappear. As you get filled with the oil of His Holy Spirit, His glorious light will turn on your whole being.

Then, your way forward will become apparent, and a life of celebrating the light of His love in you will take over and shine out. Not only to show you the way but to show others the way as well.

As Jesus said, "You are the light 0f the world. Let your light so shine" (Matthew 5:14-16).

"We have become 'children of light" (Ephesians 5:8) through Him.

If salvation was not necessary for mankind, there was no reason for Jesus Christ to die on the cross for our sins and then to be resurrected to give us eternal life. There would have been no point. The point is, spiritual salvation is a reality, and it is only through Jesus Christ (Yeshua Ha Mashiach).

Another quote, - "Live as though, Christ died yesterday, arose today and is coming back tomorrow." How should we live then? By giving it all we've got, every day as if it is our last.

CHAPTER 16

Grace Will Get You There

"For by **grace** you have been saved through faith, and that not of yourselves; it is **the gift of God**, 9. not of works, lest anyone should boast" (Ephesians 2:8-9).

GRACE, i.e., divine influence upon the heart, grace that affords joy, freely given, gratitude, pleasure, delight, sweetness, charm, loveliness: grace of speech, good will, loving-kindness, unmerited favour.

1 Corinthians 15:10 – "But by the grace of God I am what I am, and His grace toward me was not in vain; but I labored more abundantly than they all, **yet not I, but the grace of God which was with me.**

As expressed so well in these scriptures, it's not about struggling to build up grace in us through our 'works' of trying to be nice or good. We **receive grace as a gift.** The grace to endure hardship, loss, grief, rejection, resentments, insecurities, self-centeredness, etc. God's grace is the gift which keeps on giving once we receive it.

Grace is the lubrication that transforms us from a dysfunctional damaged vehicle, where the seized cogs of Godly humanity are greased into action. It is where we are transformed miraculously into highly functional human beings that are empowered to empower.

How do we get this grace to be empowered and to empower? Grace comes upon us like a magnetic attraction. A gift from God. How? Through our weaknesses and infirmities. Crying out in our hearts for God's help, to intervene on our behalf.

"And He said to me, 'My grace is sufficient for you, for My strength is made perfect in weakness. Therefore, most gladly I will rather boast in my infirmities, that the power of Christ may rest upon me' (2 Corinthians 12:9).

It is expressed well in 1Peter 5:5-7 "Likewise, you younger people, submit yourselves to your elders. Yes, all of you be **submissive** to one another, and be clothed with **humility**, for ***God resists the proud, but gives grace to the humble.*** Therefore, **humble yourselves** under the mighty hand of God, that He may exalt you in due time, **casting all your care upon Him, for He cares for you."**

These are the keys that allow us to live and function out of God's Grace. It is clear here in God's word that He gives **His grace to the humble.**

His grace is a gift. Therefore, receive it now, humble yourself before the Lord and His grace will rest upon you and empower you. Remember this gift transaction is from a place of our own weakness.

We are to submit to one another with humility and to humble ourselves under the hand of God casting our cares and concerns onto Him because He cares for each one of us.

Grace is a commodity. Grace is one of the currencies of heaven.

My wife Felicity is a woman of grace. Felicity uses this wonderful Godly currency of grace every day. The definition of the name Felicity is 'a state of bliss, happiness'.

I am the most blessed recipient because I am blessed by her smile and grace every day. She carries an air of love and acceptance; she brings this fragrant air wherever she goes. Felicity releases this calming influence which has an all-pervasive effect on all people and in any situation. She carries grace like a princess walking down the aisle. People are touched and mesmerized by God's presence in her. That is the important point to remember, it is God's presence, His gifted grace which is available for us all.

Grace comes to us as an exchange. An exchange of our cares and concerns through the price of humility before God. In Felicity's case, it was the breakup of her family at the age of fourteen. The loss of everything she knew and held dear.

She was the eldest of three siblings. Her father, due to bad choices on his part, was emotionally and physically removed from the family. The family was in distress and felt abandoned. Felicity's mother was suffering and was mentally and emotionally exhausted.

But she had three children to nurture and protect. So, she kept moving forward - even doing a Social Worker's course. She started to help others in distress and is still doing so to this day. Wendy, you are a real trooper!

Many people were praying for the family and were very supportive in their distress. Grace has the effect of being able to be passed on. In our hurt, grief, dismay and helplessness, God is there for us all, as he was for Felicity.

Around this same time, Felicity was invited to go to a crusader camp, which was a Christian outreach for youth. It was here that Felicity met Jesus as her personal Saviour and where His Grace poured into her life. His Grace poured into Felicity as a sweet-smelling fragrant scent. Christ's incense in Felicity has touched everybody else, including and especially me, ever since. The imparting fragrance of grace.

Of course, as is so often the case in the twists and turns, in the hills and valleys of distresses and traumas of this life, that God's plans and purposes come into play. Serendipity does its thing through 'God instances'. In my case I met Felicity.

When I first met Felicity, she smiled - her fragrant grace was emersed on me and melted my heart instantly. Her ability to smile into me and everybody else who experiences her grace become immediately influenced. Her penetrating smile of love and acceptance, brings with it an impartation of supernatural change.

A Godly grace that soothes, heals, and calms the soul like a soothing balm, no matter the state, manner, mood, or circumstance that we may be confronted by. A state of grace believes and trusts and supports without expecting anything in return. Grace is like a protective covering against all onslaughts of dismay or discouragement. Grace picks you up and lifts you over the abyss of despair, frustration, and distress.

When we want to give up, grace says, 'Take another step,' grace says, 'I believe in you.' Grace says, 'Don't give up'. Thank God for His grace. In my life, 'Grace' is Felicity.

This same grace is available for all of us. So, let's choose grace for each other. Let's choose to believe for the best in each other. Let grace be a total investment in each other. To see and believe in all of us, to persevere and aim to climb the mountain of hope for ourselves and each other. To believe and see and fulfil our full potential.

Grace is looking for the good in each other and trusting God's love and amazing Grace to smooth off the rough edges in each other. We, in turn, accept one another in who we are, rather than how we want each other to be.

We are to cheer each other on to the finish line of our calling and to claim our prize. The prize of "well done good and faithful servant" (Matthew 25:21).

CHAPTER 17

World Agendas-The Spirit Of This Age

Do not love the world or the things in the world. If anyone loves the world, the love of the Father is not in him. For all that is in the world—the lust of the flesh, the lust of the eyes, and the pride of life—is not of the Father but is of the world. And the world is passing away, and the lust of it; but he who does the will of God abides forever" (1 John 2:15-17).

The crises, the pain and the trauma of this life, the trials and tribulations, the death and destructions. The wars, the rumors of wars, the pestilence, the droughts, the floods, the earthquakes. They are all ongoing.

In Revelation 21:1. The apostle John speaks of a "New Heaven and a new Earth." Until that time we will have struggles.

As I have said earlier, we are in warfare on this side of heaven. Therefore, if you don't have your heavenly soldiers' uniform on, you are going to get 'knocked rotten'. Like in war, as a soldier, you are designed and equipped for the battle.

It is vital as a soldier to have 'time out', for R&R - respite and refreshing. There is always a need for God's strategies and life balance. To know what is God's battle for you and what isn't.

Waiting for God's download and timing is most important as the Lord is the commander of the army of God, in which we are a part. Warfare is about strategy. We need to be strategic every day.

Our life is a marathon with many hills and valleys. Being strategic and getting God's battle plans daily will help us pace ourselves and stay strong and vital for the long hall.

We can often be presumptuous and willful and be out of synch with God's timing and purpose. But as we wait on the lord, He will raise us up and lead us back into the fray for doing His plans and purposes (Isaiah 40:31).

The Spirit of the Lord activates these purposes. He anoints us for the task on a day-by-day basis. "To preach the gospel to the poor, to heal the brokenhearted, to set the captives free, recovery of sight to the blind, to free those who are oppressed and to proclaim the acceptable year of the Lord's favour" (Luke 4:18-19).

In all this we need to ask God daily for His wisdom and direction. He is the 'captain' of our soul.

I quite often facetiously say, "One of these days, this life is going to kill you." But more importantly, how are we living? The point being, we are all going to die physically. But what is also true is that we are spiritual beings with a spiritual destiny. We will live on in the spirit, either in God's Grace and presence or not. It is having faith in God's will and purpose, trusting him in all things with no regrets.

"Love has been perfected among us in this: that we may have boldness in the day of judgment; because as He is, so are we in this world. There is no fear in love; but perfect love casts out fear, because fear involves torment. But he who fears has not been made perfect in love. We love Him because He first loved us" (1 John 4:17-19).

Knowing and believing and trusting in God's love means that there is no need to fear. There is not even room to worry if we are full of God's love. Ask to be refreshed and filled by his love every day.

Remember, in our partnership; it is not about us performing in God. It is allowing God to perform in us. Trusting in His love is the antidote against all worldly fear.

Nothing stands out more pointedly regarding worldly fear than over the last eighteen months with the Covid 19 pandemic and the onslaught of possible death from this infection. We are all dying every day from something. In the case of covid 19, from the given statistics, it is still less than 1 percent of the population. Research says 98.8 percent of the population survives.

For all of us, there are many ways to die - I could be hit by a bus tomorrow. Should I be mindful of crossing the road? Yes. Should I worry about crossing the road? No. Should I use wisdom and be mindful of staying healthy and having good sanitation and cleanliness? Yes. Should I be constantly worried and anxious about getting sick or dying? No.

Angie, my daughter, asked me once when she was struggling to recover from adrenal fatigue, "Do you think I will live a long life?"

My answer was, "Darling, whether you are nine or ninety, this life goes real, real, real quick. And if you're spending any time worrying about it, you just wasted that time."

We all know that fear is a natural and necessary instinct for survival. But ongoing chronic anxiety is debilitating and soul-destroying, it also leads to disease through its effects on our immune system.

Angie, through her discoveries, recovering from adrenal fatigue, now checks her mind for any fears or concerns. She puts them on her visionary proverbial leaf and puts that leaf on her flowing river of goodbyes and says goodbye to those feelings. 'Good one Pange'.

My point is that living life out of chronic fear is exhausting and blocks life. Chronic fear is also the devil's playground. So don't go there.

Of course, using wisdom in decision-making is a part of why God gave us a brain. But let us make decisions based on faith rather than fear.

Faith will move you into the direction of what you have peace about or joy or a desire that keeps coming back to you.

As you go back to God and say, "But what do you say?" You can then trust in that sense as a divine lead and take your next step of faith. Faith empowers us in the right direction of decision making. Fear will do the opposite.

There is a saying I used to say to my kids, "Just do your best and let God take care of the rest."

There is the evil intent by the powers of this world, especially in the media, to further stir up this fear and catastrophize the situations in this world. It is the world's way to have more influence and control. It fuels fear and promotes more control. To isolate, to blame, to promote tribalism, disunity, and a leading towards totalitarian socialism.

The same can be said for the fear-mongering promoted by the global warming proponents. The truth is clear - there is global warming, there always has been. There will always be temperature change. It is a cyclic reality.

Geophysicists can tell you that there are many components to global warming, eg, sunspots, earth tilts, magnetic poles, solar winds, geo thermals, and much more. To suggest man can control global warming simply by reducing man-made carbon emissions, is the height of worldly impudence and arrogance.

Scientific research suggests that the percentage level of atmospheric CO_2 is .04 approximately. The man-made component of CO_2 in the atmosphere is .0016 approximately. This worldly fear and the histrionics are to bring in total control onto the world stage and bring in a world government scenario.

It is true that God gave mankind, authority and stewardship of this world. Genesis 1:26-28, "To rule over."

With the authority that we have been given, can we look after this world better? Yes. Should we look after this world better? Yes. Can we and should we reduce pollution and find better forms of energy. Yes! Can man control global warming, No!

Again, we can still give our best and trust God to take care of the rest. In Psalm 50:12 God says, "The world is mine and all its fullness."

God's word says in Genesis 8:21-22, "And the LORD smelled a soothing aroma. Then the LORD said in His heart, "I will never again curse the ground for man's sake, although the imagination of man's heart is evil from his youth; nor will I again destroy every living thing as I have done. While the earth remains, Seedtime and harvest, Cold and heat, Winter and summer, and day and night Shall not cease."

The godless powers of this world would like to think that it is in control of all things, including trying to control climate. But at the end of the day, God has all authority. It is His world. In the end, we need to be under His authority.

The hairs on our heads are numbered, including our days on this earth. Jesus said, "And do not fear those who kill the body but cannot kill the soul. But rather fear Him who is able to destroy both soul and body in hell. Are not two sparrows sold for a copper coin? And not one of them falls to the ground apart from your Father's will. But the very hairs of your head are all numbered. Do not fear; therefore, you are of more value than many sparrows" (Matthew 10:28-31).

Our confidence is in our faith. "For whatever is born of God overcomes the world. And this is the victory that has overcome the world—our faith" (1 John 5:4).

CHAPTER 18

Go with your Gut.

The terminology, 'Go with your Gut' or 'What does your gut tell you?', is a very telling form of communication. It means, listen to your inner self. It is a level of understanding, an inner knowing that comes from a deeper more sublime source than mental analysis.

Our thinking quite often can come from our own experiences, prejudices, and agendas. It will tend to lead us into a world-view mind set. This form of thinking can be very flawed by the nature from where this thinking comes from.

Tainted negative views and agendas can influence our thinking and decision-making in a destructive way. The 'vertical living' principle is to position ourselves to be open to and receive the 'mind of Christ'. The 'horizontal' direction will lead us back into being conformed to the spirit of this world.

Therefore, how can we have confidence in our gut choices? Knowing there are these opposing influences in our inner man.

Here is the principle, the blueprint, the influence, the strategy, the ultimate answer and direction to take for a 'vertical living' way of life.

"I beseech you therefore, brethren, by the <u>mercies</u> of God, that you present your bodies <u>a living</u> <u>sacrifice</u>, holy, acceptable to God, which is your reasonable service. And do <u>not be conformed</u> to this world, but be <u>transformed</u> by the <u>renewing of your mind</u>, <u>that you may prove</u> what is that good and acceptable and perfect will of God" (Romans 12:1-2).

1/ **God's mercy** - this speaks of God's 'bowels' of compassion', pity and emotional longing for us.
2/ **being a living sacrifice** - go back to the vertical and hand over all your cares and concerns, choose God's will over your own.
3/ **choose not to be conformed** to the world's view. Make a stand to honour God's boundaries. His word.
4/ **by the renewing of your mind** - Ask the Holy Spirit in Jesus Name to renew your mind.
5/ **That you may prove** - to examine, test, scrutinize and discern. Step back and view the situation and ask God, "But what do you say Lord?" See things from the third person, God's perspective. Be assured, better choices will be made.

These five points will give you complete confidence to **BELIEVE** that going with the '**GUT**' will be God's lead for you.

This leads you back into the '**God Equation**', which is **BELIEF + ACTION = FAITH.** Use this equation for life.

"For who has known the mind of the LORD that he may instruct Him? But we have the mind of Christ" (1 Corinthians 2:16.).

I believe the 'gut' instinct comes from a mixture of different benevolent supports - God's grace, the leading of the Holy Spirit and angelic influences.

Of course, there are opposing influences as well - the bad bugs of the gut. In a spiritual context, these are the demonic hordes that try to dominate and inflame our being. Their purpose is to cause disruption,

GO WITH YOUR GUT.

damage, and trauma to our inner man. To lead us down the wrong path towards destruction.

Physically an inflamed condition of the gut can lead to what's called a "leaky gut syndrome". This condition allows toxins to enter our blood stream and damages the whole body.

There is an ongoing continuum between our spiritual gut and our physical gut.

As mentioned before, my daughter Angie is now studying medical science. This study will lead her into becoming a health practitioner.

This desire came from her experiences as she went through her own health crises after her immune system crashed. It came about after working long, stressful hours over many years as a TV producer.

Angie started to learn more about the nature of negative stress on the human body its effects on the digestive system and how this breakdown can lead to many allergic conditions. Her interests started to turn to the 'microbiome' system of the gastrointestinal system ie, 'gut bacteria'.

There are trillions of gut bacteria, i.e., 'bug's', in our gastrointestinal system. Some are good for us some are not.

Bad bacteria (bugs) can thrive if allowed, through bad eating choices, i.e., <u>what</u> we take in. It's also important <u>how</u> we take food in. Are we relaxed or under stress? Are we rushing around or at peace?

In my work as an Osteopath, I have seen many instances where gastrointestinal inflammation will make the nervous system sensitive. This, in turn, leads to muscle spasming and joint stress. This is termed a 'viscero-somatic reflex'.

In like manner, an irritable nervous system can also cause an irritable gut. It is due to the sympathetic nervous system activating the adrenal gland for a 'fight and flight' response. This sympathetic system is designed for our survival. This system will override the parasympathetic nervous system, which was designed for our assimilation and digestion.

The parasympathetic nervous system will enhance blood flow to the gut. If this system is overridden, this imbalance will reduce blood flow, which is our life resource to the GIT. i.e; the 'gastrointestinal tract'

"The life of the flesh is in the blood" (Leviticus 17:11). It will affect digestion, which can lead to the many GIT diseases.

I will always say to patients, "if you cannot eat restfully, don't eat" So, the question is what are we taking into our 'belly', and how is our gut receiving it?

"If anyone thirsts, let him come to Me and drink. He who believes in Me, as the Scripture has said, out of his heart (belly) will flow rivers of living water" (John 7:37-38).

So, the question is in this life, what are we thirsting for? What are we ingesting? Jesus spoke of himself being living water. He also stated he was the bread of life.

"And Jesus said to them, 'I am the bread of life. He who comes to Me shall never hunger, and he who believes in Me shall never thirst' (John 6:35).

Where are we getting our life resources? In this scripture, Jesus says, 'I am your life-giving resource.

Jesus is saying, "I will fill you. I will refresh you. I will produce life in you. I will produce health in you. Then my life in you will pour out of you and produce life in others." This is the way of true life - this is the way we are designed to live and function.

To be empowered to empower - to drink in every day the life resource of Jesus Christ. Through drinking in the fullness of His Holy Spirit – this is empowerment. Anything else that we may take into our heart, or in this case our 'belly', will cause literal distention and dissension, physically and spiritually.

We will literally bloat with the pressure of this world, expanding in us it's toxic residue. As we become more toxic from this nauseating resource, we will eventually spew it out over ourselves and others around us. Nobody likes to be sick and nauseous.

Two years ago, I had my first real experience of being sick. Out of the blue, I came down with influenza A and double pneumonia. In the process, I blacked out and was taken by ambulance to hospital. I had to stay there a week until my temperature went down, and my oxygen levels went up. I knew when my oxygen levels went down because I could feel this awful debilitating nausea start to take over. It was the worst feeling. The medication I had been on wasn't working.

I felt led by the Lord to ring up some prayer warrior friends to pray for me. At the same time, I felt led to confess and repent for an earlier event a few months prior, where I believe I took on a spirit of fear caused by an accusing spirit. The next morning the medical team changed meds, and within hours, I started to recover. That nausea was the worst, I never want to go down that track again. Thank you, Lord.

DON'T GET ISOLATED, IT WILL MAKE YOU SICK

My only other time of nausea was going away with friends after finishing my high school leaving exams. My friends and I went down to this cabin near a secluded beach in the national park. Warning, don't get or stay isolated in this life. Not being connected with good people around you is dangerous for your health. Unfortunately, my decision at the age of seventeen was limited.

I took down a bottle of Bacardi and some coca-cola. My so-called friends played a trick on me and filled a large glass with Bacardi and colored it with the cola. As this night progressed, the nauseating side effects to my 'gut' took over.

The principle of whatever you do in this life - there is always a price to be paid, took over. This price took the form of alcoholic poisoning. It came in the form of bringing up bright yellow bile all night.

Crawling down to the beach the next morning, I was delighted to feel the warm sunshine on my face. Knowing I had survived my toxic experience was a real relief, even though it did take time for my 'gut' to recover. But a good lesson learned.

Let The light of Jesus shine onto your face. All you have to do is, look up to him. He is the 'author and finisher 'of life.

"Looking unto Jesus, the author and finisher of our faith, who for the joy that was set before Him endured the cross, despising the shame, and has sat down at the right hand of the throne of God" (Hebrews 12:2).

Ps: It has been 48 years since that incident, and I have never had Bacardi since.

In this life, drink only from Jesus and let Him be your pure resource. Everything else is not suitable for our design. But like the Bacardi, like all the stimulants of this world, they are counterfeit resources. They will lead you into a toxic milieu of distress, ongoing nausea, and chronic damage with eternal consequences.

Like any addiction, once we are lured into the supposed sweetness of this worldly life, it is hard to break the habit to our soul. It is like trying to get off sugar. It takes all our will to beat the addiction. But once you do, you realize how toxic and damaging the sugar was to your 'gut' and to your body as a whole.

Be determined to beat the toxic intake of the temptations of this world. So, go with your 'GUT'. Go to God. Let His healing grace overtake you. Breathe in the oxygen of His Holy Spirit. Get determined to drink in Christ - His healing waters will take over as a supernatural tonic and medicine.

CHAPTER 19

From Faith To Faith

As an Osteopath I have treated patients with muscle damage for many years. Muscles need to be exercised, so they are stronger than the load that is coming against them. If the discipline of exercise is maintained, we stay more robust than the load, and no damage occurs to our body. If we keep exercising, we build more muscle.

The same principle is in play for our faith muscle. As scripture says, we go from 'Strength to strength'. As said before, 'If we don't use it, we lose it'. Like losing physical muscle, if we stop using our faith muscle, we will set ourselves up for some damage.

Another scripture says, "For whatever is not from faith is sin" (Romans 14:23). Woah! Remember, sin means we are off target. We need spiritual faith muscles to stay on target. To go God's way and not our way or somebody else's. Target our faith in God for ourselves, faith for our loved ones, faith for our friends, faith for our co-workers. Acting on our beliefs creates faith in action, which pleases God.

"But without faith it is impossible to please Him, for he who comes to God must believe that He is, and that He is a rewarder of those who diligently seek Him" (Hebrews 11:6).

So, whatever is going on in your life, recalibrate your thought processing and go back to faith through partnering God. Hand over all your concerns and ask and receive God's download, then get back on target.

This trust is your daily requirement to get back on track and move forwards in this journey of faith. Faith in our designer, our design, each other, and faith in God's lead, plan and purpose. Even on those difficult days, trust in the Lord, and cast your cares upon Him. He won't leave you or forsake you.

Let's stay faithful to the call of Jesus. Let's back up our mate and please Him, like the Anzacs in the trenches of life. Trust in your mate next to you, your mate Jesus. "For in it, (THE GOSPEL) the righteousness of God is revealed from faith to faith; as it is written, "The just shall live by faith" Romans 1:17.

God is faithful, and His faithfulness is revealed. It means to uncover what has been covered or veiled, disclose and reveal, and make known. From 'faith to faith' means what is revealed to us is an ongoing process. "Like layer upon layer, line upon line, precept upon precept, here a little there a little" (Isaiah 68:13).

So, we learn and grow through this journey of life, a little at a time. The principle of this growth is expressed well in (Romans 5:1-4) "Therefore, having been justified by faith, we have peace with God through our Lord Jesus Christ, through whom also we have access by faith into this grace in which we stand, and rejoice in hope of the glory of God. And not only that, but we also glory in tribulations, knowing that tribulation produces perseverance; and perseverance, character; and character, hope."

Tribulation's, perseverance, character, and hope! Yes, we grow in faith through doing the hard yards of life. Where we are taken out of our comfort zones and put into places of our weaknesses and helplessness - in these places, we can't rely on ourselves.

But it is in these places of tribulation that our character in Christ grows. From strength to strength and glory to glory. As our character develops through the hard yards of faith, so do the blessings.

I remember a time when Felicity and I went with friends to Phnom Penh. On our first day of what we thought would be a 'relaxing' holiday, our friends went to visit the dentist. While they were at the dentist, we decided to exchange some cash and explore the city. We had a map with us and figured we could get around ok and work out directions. We were in control, haha, not!

Within half an hour, we had gone from gentle, quiet suburbia into the dark bowels of a foreign metropolis that was frightfully unfamiliar. We had walked into the central marketplace of the city. This market had been designed like a huge sprawling octagon with eight different ways in and out. We went in one way, and after pushing through stifling heat and maddening crowds, we then ventured out by way of another exit. The streets crisscrossed in all directions. The map we had and the streets we were looking at didn't match at all.

We started to show people our map to try and get new bearings, but nobody there read maps to our dismay. Not only that but they were also directing us to go in all sorts of wrong directions.

Suddenly we realized that we were lost in the middle of Phnom Phen. We walked and walked, trying to find a street that would lead us back to the serenity and the safety of our hotel, but to no avail.

Felicity was getting exhausted, struggling under the oppressive heat and the compressing crowds. I did not know what to do next. It was like being caught in another rip of being out of control and desperate. Just like I was years ago with Jeremy in the surf.

This time the current pulling us was the tidal rush of a foreign city sucking the lifeblood out of us. A sense of helpless desperation started to take over. Once again, I said to God, "What are we going to do?"

Then, out of the blue, we heard a voice behind us saying in perfect English, "Can I help you?" This lady was a local. She was immaculately dressed and carried such a presence of peace and assuredness that I believe she must have been an angel sent by God to take us out of this place of trauma and helplessness. She was, and she did! She looked at the map and motioned to a man standing next to a Tuk Tuk. She spoke to him and gave him the proper directions. We hopped in this Tuk Tuk, which was also a first for us. We looked around to say thank you, and she was gone. She had literally vanished. Woah!

The elation of getting back to our hotel and soaking in the hotel pool, which I call 'the pool of thanksgiving', will never be forgotten. Nor will we ever forget what we believe was a visitation by a physical angel on a Godly mission on our behalf. Thankyou.

The moral of the story is that getting to the end of ourselves is where faith starts and where God meets us. Yes, this life of ours, is an ongoing process of going and growing from 'faith to faith'. From strength to strength. From glory to glory. Precept to precept and line upon line.

WOW, WOW, WOW.

On a different faith note - recently in my clinic, a lady brought in her sixteen-year-old daughter. They were recommended to see me by a youth pastor. The daughter, three years earlier, had fallen off a twenty-three-meter cliff. The daughter explained that as she was falling, she believed that she would survive.

As with many traumas in life, there is always a price to be paid. Life is full of consequences and side effects.

But the price that Jesus paid for us comes into the equation of life's traumas as well. Where his grace gives us the capacity to cope, to persevere and endure the hardships from the fallouts of life. He bridges the gaps for us and gives us the capacity to not only carry on but to pass it on and help others do the same. Again, "the comfort we are comforted with will comfort others".

This sixteen-year-old girl had suffered many fractures and contusions. All traumas of life can have chronic side affects, some physical, some emotional and spiritual. In her case, through my examination, I was able to show her and show her mother that she was suffering a marked spinal scoliosis, i.e., 'spinal curvature'. On laying her on the examination table I noticed a discernable difference in her leg length. Her right femur was two centimeters shorter than her left femur. This short right leg was caused by the trauma to her boney growth plates due to the fall three years earlier.

I showed them both the leg length discrepancy. The daughter was quite impressed with having a short leg and said, "Wow! I've got a short leg."

I said to her, "Why don't we pray for healing?" She agreed. Remembering that God's word says, "To lay hands on the sick and they will recover" (Mark 16:17-18). Also, when you pray, have faith, believe and do not doubt. (Matthew 20:21-22) and miracles can happen.

We finished praying. She looked up at me and said, "I could feel something happening in my body." She also said, "I don't usually listen that well, but I heard every word you said."

I smiled and said that was great. Then I said, "Let's sit you up and look at your leg length." As she sat up, she looked with her eyes wide open and cried, "WOW! WOW! WOW!"

Her ankle bones from being uneven by two centimeters were perfectly even.

I explained, "You came here in faith. I am here in faith. We pray in faith without doubting, knowing that God is faithful and faithful to His word."

God's timing and our timing might be different for many of us. God's eternal plans and purpose are higher than ours. But let us always remember that God loves each one of us and He is always faithful and true to His word and to us.

As He is faithful let us stay faithful to Him. He is the 'Alpha and Omega'.

After this miraculous event, I was still treating her connective tissue condition and muscular guarding. She looked up at me and asked, "What about my back?"

I told her, "That will also be straight."

She asked, "Really?"

I said, "Stand up and have a look."

Her response again, "WOW, WOW, WOW!" Sure enough, totally healed and whole in Jesus' name.

Trust in God's word in your heart and over your life. Hold on and never let go. As you press into God, His love and power will press into you like a spiritual atomic reaction. Watch His power being released in you and through you. That's His promise.

(Mark 11:23-24) "For assuredly, I say to you, Whoever says to this mountain, 'Be removed and cast into the sea,' and does not doubt in his heart, but believes that those things he says will be done, he will have whatever he says.

"Therefore I say to you, whatever things you ask when you pray, believe that you receive them, and you will have them."

PRAY THEY WILL GET A GUILTY CONSCIENCE

This prayer was a fervent prayer said by Felicity after losing her wedding ring, engagement ring and eternity ring in one go. Her rings were attached together.

On this certain day due to her rings feeling too tight on her wedding finger, she decided to take them off and put them on her little finger. They seemed to look a bit loose on her little finger.

I said to her, be careful, they may fall off.

We had been out all day and had visited many places.

That night Felicity looked at her hand and gasped, "My rings are gone!"

We were at a friends place and we agreed to pray and believe for Felicity's rings to be returned.

Felicity's fervent prayer was from a real place of belief and not doubting, Her prayer was that, 'whoever found her rings would get a guilty concience and would hand them in'.

Felicity put her belief into action and went down to the police station and gave them a description of her rings.

One year later we get a phone call from the police station, stating, "We believe we have your rings!" Yes they were Felicity's lost rings.

They had been handed in at 1:00am on a Saturday morning, there was a note saying that the rings had been found in a car park a year earlier.

The police said this doesn't ever happen. But we know that God knows better.

(James 5:16) "The effective, fervent prayer of a righteous man avails much." Another great example of faith enacted on by a prayer of faith, believing and not doubting. In this, mountains move and rings are miraculously found.

Good job Felicity, good job God.

You see whether it was Felicity and myself at the end of ourselves, helpless but not hopeless in the distress of being lost in a foreign city, or a patient in ongoing pain and discomfort with no relief in sight. To know without a doubt that God is always faithful and His loving grace will always meet our needs.

"My grace is sufficient for you, for my strength is made perfect in weakness" (2 Corinthians 12:9). This is the reality of our life. No matter the circumstance, God is always there for us and will always meet us from a position of faith and love, a position of believing and not doubting. The position of **THE VERTICAL.** For it is not only faith in Christ but also the faith in Christ in us. "Most assuredly, I say to you, he who believes in Me, the works that I do he will do also; and greater works than these he will do, because I go to My Father. And whatever you ask in My name, that I will do, that the Father may be glorified in the Son. If you ask anything in My name, I will do it" (John 14:12-14). This is the promise of God for all of us for life.

The gifts of the Holy Spirit were given to us, to all who want to receive. Reach out and receive the love of Christ afresh in your heart. Ask and receive by faith for the infilling of His Holy Spirit.

Ask, Believe and Receive. Do not doubt and say thank you.

CHAPTER 20

Celebration

It's time to celebrate. Life is to be celebrated. But why should we celebrate when life can be so devastatingly traumatic, painful and grief-ridden?

Because of the promises of God's word and the promises of Jesus.

"If then you were raised with Christ, seek those things which are above, where Christ is, sitting at the right hand of God. Set your mind on things above, not on things on the earth. For you died, and your life is hidden with Christ in God. When Christ who is our life appears, then you also will appear with Him in glory" (Colossians 3:1-4).

So, to paraphrase God's word. He is saying that even though we are still living in this mortal coil with all the pains and traumas that go with this life, God says, if we die to the things of this world and live for Christ, we then identify more with the things that are above. We identify with the things of our destiny, the things that are eternal, the things that are of Christ and through Christ. As we do this and endure the pains of this world through this exchanged life, we can truly celebrate this life daily despite all the traumas and pains that go with it.

You see, there is so much historical evidence of the reality of the life and times of Jesus that the most ardent denier of Christ would be put to shame. Unfortunately, most deniers, by their own willful nature, choose not to see the truth. So, that black is white, and white is black. Keep praying for them. But with truth in place, the quality of the man Jesus and what He said and what He did is clear for all to see.

So, the argument is straightforward, either Jesus was a liar, a lunatic, or He was exactly who He said He was. God the son, the Christ, the Messiah, Lord, and Saviour of the world. In this the only option for all of us is to accept him as Lord or reject Him. You choose. Jesus gave us the right to become sons of God.

"But as many as received Him, to them He gave the right to become children of God, to those who believe in His name: who were born, not of blood, nor of the will of the flesh, nor of the will of man, but of God" (John 1:12-13).

For the promises of God are yes and amen. (2 Corinthians 1:20). God's promises to us are an eternal contract that can never be broken. So, we celebrate from a position of belief in God's promises to us through Jesus.

The Bible tells us that, "Looking unto Jesus, the author, and finisher of our faith, who for the joy that was set before Him endured the cross, despising the shame, and has sat down at the right hand of the throne of God" (Hebrews 12:2).

Yes, Jesus is our greatest example of belief and faith in action. He endured the pain, the grief, the sicknesses, and the sorrows of the world. He endured it all for us. But it doesn't mean we don't suffer the pains, griefs sicknesses and sorrows of this world ourselves.

But the point of the celebration is that Jesus is with us, helping and empowering us through the pains of this world. This is the empowering reality given to us by Jesus for all who receive the Holy Spirit of God.

CELEBRATION

It is what empowers us, not so much to avoid the pain and hardships of this world but to overcome them.

His word says, "Who shall separate us from the love of Christ? Shall tribulation, or distress, or persecution, or famine, or nakedness, or peril, or sword? As it is written:For Your sake we are killed all day long; We are accounted as sheep for the slaughter. Yet in all these things we are more than conquerors through Him who loved us. For I am persuaded that neither death nor life, nor angels nor principalities nor powers, nor things present nor things to come, nor height nor depth, nor any other created thing, shall be able to separate us from the love of God which is in Christ Jesus our Lord" (Romans 8:35-39).

OH, THE PAIN

As mentioned, there was a time in my life when I had blood poisoning in my leg, and I was in hospital for ten days.

Years ago, before the saving grace of antibiotics had arrived, I would have had my leg chopped off or I would have just died. But I survived without losing my leg. That's certainly worthy of celebration.

I do remember the pain I was going through. My leg was so swollen that I could see my face reflecting off my skin. I could not even get my leg to a horizontal position, let alone trying to get out of bed due to the pain of the swelling.

I vividly remember during that agonizing pain that I started to give thanks. This positioning of thanksgiving activated a supernatural download of pain relief. It helped me cope with the physical and emotional pains of life and still does now.

You see, in those moments of pain, whether physical or emotional, I realized that everything in my life at that moment had faded away into the distance. The only thing I knew was that Jesus was with me. He was all I had left, and I knew that He was enough to get me through. Either in this life or the life to come.

As I started giving thanks and praising God, I realized that I was giving thanks and, in essence, celebrating my life, not because of my circumstances, but because God was with me in my situation. As I kept saying, "Thank you Lord Jesus," I fell asleep. I woke up with a peace that went beyond all understanding and with reduced pain.

That is still my pain mantra today, "Thank you Lord Jesus" - no matter what type of pain I'm feeling. It is my faith prescription that always makes a difference. You see His word says, "I will never leave you or forsake you" (Hebrews 13:5). Also in Matthew 28:20 Jesus last words were, "And lo, I am with you always, even to the end of the age." Amen.

Jesus also says in 2 Corinthians 12:9, "My grace is sufficient for you, for My strength is made perfect in weakness. Therefore, most gladly I will rather boast in my infirmities, that the power of Christ may rest upon me."

So, in marked pain but still in faith, I started to give thanks and praising God for who He is and what He has done and what he will do. One of my favorite prescriptions as an Osteopath is to say to my patients, "Say thank you Lord Jesus, 15 times in 10 seconds every hour." Haha, I haven't quite achieved it yet but I'm still working on it, you try it.

Another reason to celebrate is that in all situations, God always 'has our backs'. Spiritually and physically. As God has 'our back', we can rejoice that we are empowered and equipped to have each other's backs.

You see, God goes before us, supports us, and hedges us from behind. Meaning that he protects us from the things that are unseen, things that we may not be aware of. The unknowns that we can't put a handle on. The "what if's" of life.

When the children of Israel were moving into their freedom through the promises of God spoken to them through Moses, they, in their pain and distress, soon quickly forgot God's promises. The Egyptians started to come after them. Fear, resentment, blame, and bitterness quickly took over in the hearts of the children of Israel. They could only see their impending doom from their carnal (flesh) perspective. They had quickly forgotten what God had already done for them.

God said to Moses in Exodus 14:14-15, "The Lord will fight for you." He also said to Moses, "Don't cry out to me lift up your rod and stretch out your hand."

It means that no matter what the situation is, or the circumstances of life are, move out in your authority, speak into the situation and use the power that you have through the anointing of the Holy Spirit, which was given to you. Speak out in your God-given authority into your life and the lives of your loved ones and the lives of the ones God has put you in charge over and for those who have charge over you.In verse 19 it says, "The Angel of the Lord who went before the camp, moved and went behind them."

God not only goes before us to prepare the way, but He also becomes our 'rear guard', supporting and protecting us from the evil onslaughts that are around us and behind us. Things that we can't control. The negative influences that we may not see or discern.

Like the children of Israel, we also can get caught up with similar attitudes. Rather than celebrating, we too, can get caught up with attitudes of complaining and blaming.

The key to breaking this awful cycle is to keep moving back into thanksgiving, celebrating and giving thanks for what we have. Rather than complaining about our circumstances and what we don't have.

As Moses stepped out in faith, The seas parted, and the Israelites moved forward into their freedom, and the enemy was taken out by God. He fights for us and has won the victory of life for us already.

"We are more than conquerors." This empowering happens in the spiritual relm and the natural. So, believe it and act on it for yourself and each other. Soon you will start to celebrate life rather than complaining and bemoaning life.

Celebration for life brings a whole myriad of different colors of celebration in your life that wasn't there before. It brings us from the darkness of anxiety and depression to the bright colors of peace and joy.

So then, let us start giving thanks and celebrate what we have in Christ, celebrate God's love and promises to us. The catalyst for a heart of celebration will always come through **belief, hope trust and faith.**

We **believe** in God's word, which moves us into **hope** for our future. We then choose to **trust** in God's word and His promises despite our feelings and situation. It moves us to finish this belief position by stepping out in **faith** and to 'having a go', day in and day out.

This is the celebration epitaph of Jesus for our lives "He is despised and rejected by men, a man of sorrows and acquainted with grief. And we hid, as it were, our faces from Him; He was despised, and we did not esteem Him. Surely, He has borne our grief; And carried our sorrows; Yet we esteemed Him stricken, smitten by God, and afflicted. But He was wounded for our transgressions, He was bruised for our iniquities; The chastisement for our peace was upon Him, And by His stripes we are healed" Isaiah 53:3-5.

The Lord had put himself in that position to protect us. He took all grief and trauma upon himself, He gave us such a knowledge of confidence and safety, even in the very difficult situations of all forms of pain and grief and sorrow.

Whether it is the loss of a job, a damaged relationship or reputation, the loss of a loved one, or whether it's a sense of uncertainty for the future. We can still celebrate life in all its fullness because of God's proactive position of love. He always goes before us and supports us from behind.

He has taken it all. All we need to do is continue to give thanks and continue to celebrate. **"For you shall not go out with haste, nor go by**

CELEBRATION

flight; For the LORD will go before you, And the God of Israel will be your rear guard" (Isaiah 52:12).

"Now may the God of hope fill you with all joy and peace in believing, that you may abound in hope by the power of the Holy Spirit" (Romans 15:13).

We can also celebrate life from this position of confidence by having each other's backs. We can have the capacity to then back each other up. To cover and support one another in life's difficulties with the same support that God gives us. Now that is worthy of celebration.

From this position of having each other's backs God's word says in **Isaiah 58:8, "Then your light shall break forth like the morning, your healing shall spring forth speedily, and your righteousness shall go before you; <u>The glory of the LORD shall be your rear guard.</u>** "What a great reason to celebrate. His life in us and our life in Him.

As we start to get into the habit of celebrating life rather than worrying about it, let's remember some of these life protocols.

Here and now, let this scripture be your mantra.

"For I determined, not to know anything among you except Jesus Christ and him crucified" (1Corinthians 2:2).

You will see the love and life of Christ be your true living water that will continually refresh, nourish and bring healing to you and all those who you meet.

For all this, go back to the 'vertical' throughout the day. Give thanks and celebrate every day. Reset yourself and be refreshed in the Prince and Princess position. Give over all your cares and concerns to the Lord your God. For He is your business partner for life. Say afresh, whatever the circumstance, "Thankyou Lord, I give it to you." Also say, "What do you say Lord?" and "What are we doing now?"

Then let the Lord lead you in this amazing journey of His love and life, then take your next step of faith in your Prince and Princess position and let 'Vertical Living' be your eternal position.

AMEN.

www.ingramcontent.com/pod-product-compliance
Lightning Source LLC
Chambersburg PA
CBHW060537100426
42743CB00009B/1552